Simple Psalter

for Year A

J. Michael Joncas

LITURGICAL PRESS
Collegeville, Minnesota

www.litpress.org

ACKNOWLEDGMENTS

Cover design: Tara Wiese. Photo courtesy of Getty Images.

The English translation of Psalm Responses from *Lectionary for Mass* © 1969, 1981, 1997, International Commission on English in the Liturgy Corporation. All rights reserved.

Verse texts from *The Abbey Psalms and Canticles* by the Monks of Conception Abbey, © 2018, 2010, United States Conference of Catholic Bishops. All rights reserved.

© 2022 The Jan Michael Joncas Trust
Published by Liturgical Press, Collegeville, Minnesota. All rights reserved. No part of this book may be used or reproduced in any manner whatsoever except brief quotations in reviews, without the written permission of Liturgical Press, Saint John's Abbey, PO Box 7500, Collegeville, MN 56321-7500. Printed in the United States of America.

ISBN: 978-0-8146-6777-4   ISBN: 978-0-8146-6778-1 (e-book)

Contents

Psalms for feast days and solemnities, such as Christmas and Easter, can be found in *Simple Psalter for Solemnities, Feasts, and Other Celebrations*. Available at www.litpress.org.

Composer's Notes

My "simple psalms" project is intended to help worshiping communities with limited musical resources to sing the appointed Responsorial Psalm for the Sundays and Holydays of the Liturgical Year. I have set the texts as they appear in the English-language *Lectionary for Mass, Second Typical Edition* (1998) (antiphons) and the *Abbey Psalms and Canticles* (verses). All of the antiphons are set metrically (i.e., not in the free rhythm of chant) because I believe that in most cases in the English-speaking world this makes their texts more memorable and easier to sing for the assembly. The verses are set to rhythmic psalm-tones similar to those of Gelineau psalmody (i.e., speech-rhythm settings of the text over pulsed accompaniment ["sprung rhythm"]). Unlike the published Gelineau psalms, however, I have notated the way I propose that the texts to be sung since I find that it is sometimes difficult for cantors to sing the Gelineau tones as notated using only whole notes. A suggested tempo appears at the beginning of each psalm as a metronome mark; this tempo can be adjusted depending on the acoustic properties of the space in which the liturgy is celebrated.

Tones are assigned to each psalm based on the genre (*Gattung*) of the psalm-text, following the pattern of my friend and colleague, Art Zannoni, as follows:

Tone 1A: Hymn of Praise, Motivation from Nature

Tone 1B: Hymn of Praise, Motivation from History or Torah

Tone 1C: Song of Zion

Tone 1D: Processional

Tone 1E: Hymn of Praise to YHWH as King

Tone 2A: Royal Coronation or Anniversary

Tone 2C: Royal Song of Thanksgiving

Tone 2D: Royal Marriage Song

Tone 3: Prophetic Psalm

Tone 4A: Community Lament

Tone 4B: Individual Lament

Tone 4C: Prayer for the Sick

Tone 5A: Communal Thanksgiving

Tone 5B: Individual Thanksgiving

Tone 6: Psalm of Confidence

Tone 8A: Wisdom Psalm 1

Tone 8B: Wisdom Psalm 2

(Missing tone numbers indicate a psalm-genre that does not appear in the Sunday and Solemnity Lectionary.)

I would here like to acknowledge the influence of three church composers whose psalm settings have influenced this project. I have already mentioned Fr. Joseph Gelineau, S.J., whose groundbreaking creation of "pulsed" psalm-tones set to sprung-rhythm texts made one of the metrical characteristics of Hebrew biblical psalms and canticles available for vernacular singing. A second influence was Howard Hughes, S.M., whose assigning of particular tones to particular genres of psalms based in contemporary form-critical analysis of the psalm-texts, has been eye- and ear-opening for me. Finally Paul Inwood was the first to call my attention to the idea of "psalm tunes" (rather than "psalm tones"). He showed how many English-language folk songs adjusted the fundamental melodic curves of their tones, eliding some syllables while assigning multiple notes to a single syllable based on the number of syllables needed.

Following the practice articulated in the *Lectionary for Mass*, these Responsorial Psalms would be performed as follows. After a period of silence to reflect on the previous scriptural reading proclaimed, a keyboard (or melody instrument) would play the melody for the Antiphon alone. The cantor would immediately intone the Antiphon with a keyboard providing accompaniment, if needed. The assembly would then repeat the Antiphon with a keyboard (and optionally other instruments) providing accompaniment, if needed. The cantor would then sing the assigned psalm verses with the assembly repeating the Antiphon after each verse.

While I believe these "simple psalms" can effectively be sung *a cappella* or with simple keyboard accompaniment, some communities might want to enhance their singing of the Responsorial Psalm with more elaborate music.

The optional harmony additions to the antiphons can be performed in a multitude of ways.

Vocally, the harmonies:

1) might be sung by soloists with the rest of the choir singing the antiphon in unison with the assembly.

2) might be sung by the soprano and alto sections of the choir with the men singing the antiphon in unison with the assembly.

3) If an SATB texture is desired, the soprano and bass sections sing the antiphon in unison with the assembly, with the tenors singing the higher harmonies an octave lower than written and the altos singing the lower harmonies as notated.

Instrumentally,

1) the SA harmonies might be played by C treble wind or string instruments, either as notated or an octave higher depending on where it best fits the instruments' tessitura.

2) the keyboardist should keep the pulse constant under the singing of the verses, but might repeat the chords as quarter notes rather than half notes, or even arpeggiate the chords as eighth notes if desired.

My preference is that the Verses be sung by a solo cantorial voice since that seems to ensure that the psalm-text be clearly sung and understood. Most of the time I have set the psalm-text for two phrases on one breath; the cantor should feel free to take a breath at an appropriate place if singing both phrases on one breath is too taxing. It is also possible to alternate male and female solo voices on the Verses, possibly with both singing the final Verse in octaves. It would also be possible to have the choir sing the verses (or just the final Verse) in unison, as long as their articulation keeps the psalm-text intelligible.

As the *Lectionary for Mass* reminds us: "The working of the Holy Spirit is needed if the word of God is to make what we hear outwardly have its effect inwardly. Because of the Holy Spirit's inspiration and support, the word of God becomes the foundation of the liturgical celebration and the rule and support of all our life. The working of the Holy Spirit precedes, accompanies and brings to completion the whole celebration of the Liturgy. But the Spirit also brings home to each person individually everything that in the proclamation of the word of God is spoken for the good of the whole gathering of the faithful" [9]. I pray that my musical settings of these "simple psalms" may help Christ's faithful, individually and collectively, hear the word of God and put it into practice in their lives. *Soli Deo gloria.*

(Fr. Jan) Michael Joncas
St. Paul, MN

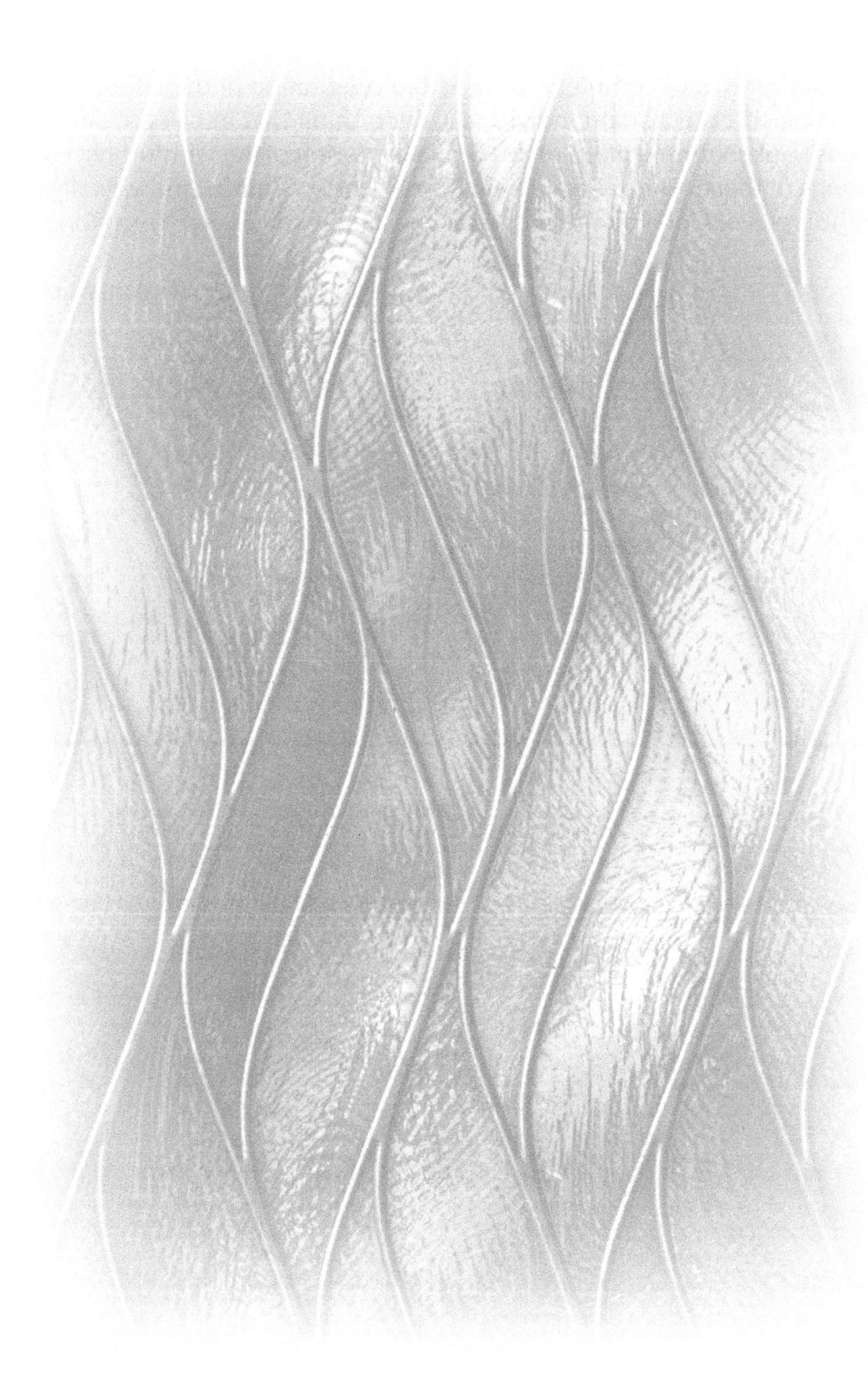

Psalm 122: Let Us Go Rejoicing
First Sunday of Advent, Year A

Psalm 122:1-2, 3-4, 4-5, 6-7, 8-9

Michael Joncas
Tone 1C: Song of Zion

First Sunday of Advent, Year A

First Sunday of Advent, Year A

First Sunday of Advent, Year A

sake of the house of the LORD, our God, I will seek good things for you.

Psalm 72: Justice Shall Flourish
Second Sunday of Advent, Year A

Psalm 72:1-2, 7-8, 12-13, 17

Michael Joncas
Tone 5B: Individual Thanksgiving

Second Sunday of Advent, Year A

Second Sunday of Advent, Year A

Psalm 146: Lord, Come and Save Us
Third Sunday of Advent, Year A

Psalm 146:6-7, 8-9, 9-10

Michael Joncas
Tone 4B: Individual Lament

Third Sunday of Advent, Year A

Third Sunday of Advent, Year A

Third Sunday of Advent, Year A

Psalm 24: Let the King Enter
Fourth Sunday of Advent, Year A

Psalm 24:1-2, 3-4, 5-6

Michael Joncas
Tone 1D: Processional

Fourth Sunday of Advent, Year A

Fourth Sunday of Advent, Year A

Ant.

hands   and pure   of   heart,   whose soul   is not set   on   vain things.

F   E⁷   Am   F   C   G^SUS4   G

Verse 3

3. Bless-ings from the LORD shall he re - ceive,   and right re - ward from the God who saves him.

Cmaj⁷   F   G^SUS4   G   F   G   C^SUS4   C

Ant.

Such are the peo-ple who   seek him,   who seek the face of the God of   Ja - cob.

F   E⁷   Am   F   C   G^SUS4   G

Psalm 128: Blessed Are Those
The Holy Family of Jesus, Mary, and Joseph, Years A, B, and C

Psalm 128:1-2, 3, 4-5

Michael Joncas
Tone 8B: Wisdom Psalm 2

The Holy Family of Jesus, Mary, and Joseph, Years A, B, and C

The Holy Family of Jesus, Mary, and Joseph, Years A, B, and C

Psalm 29: The Lord Will Bless
The Baptism of the Lord, Years A, B, and C

Psalm 29:1-2, 3-4, 9-10

Michael Joncas
Tone 1A: Hymn of Praise
Motivation from Nature

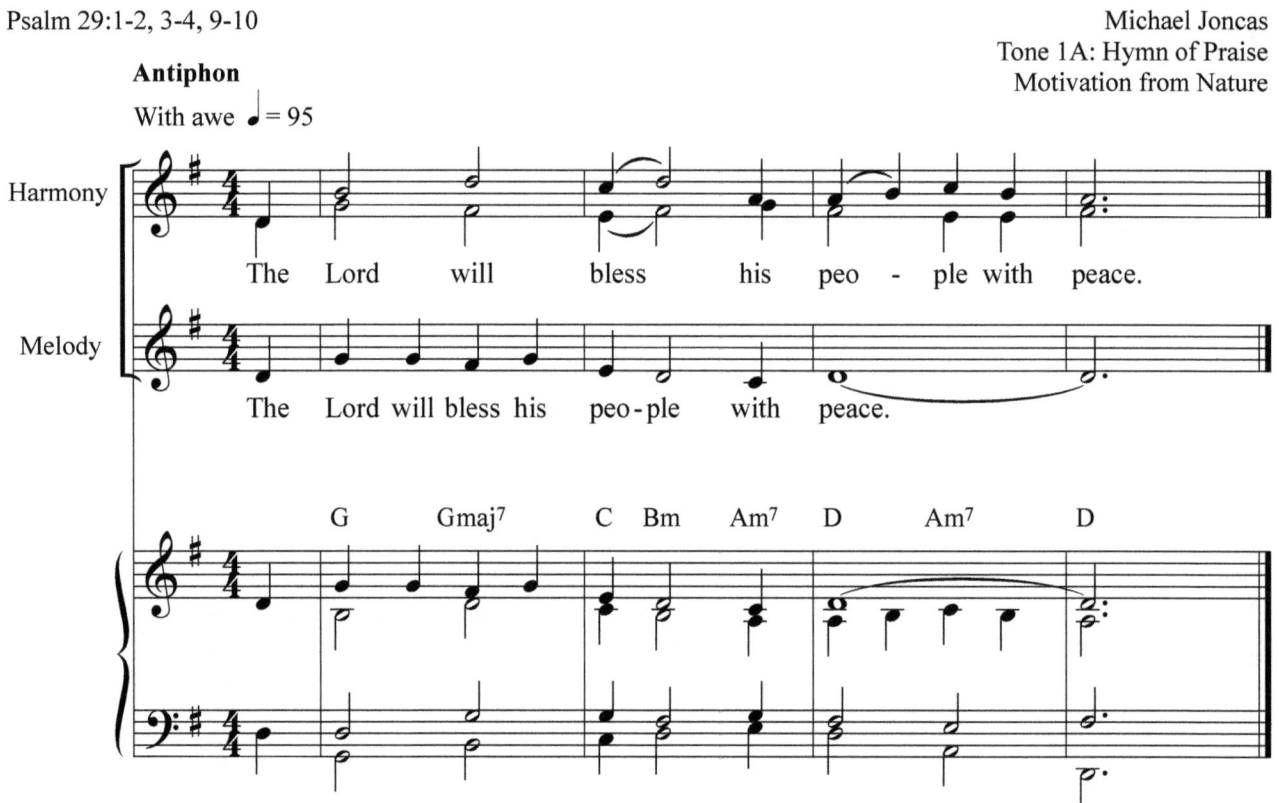

The Baptism of the Lord, Years A, B, and C

The Baptism of the Lord, Years A, B, and C

Ant.

power;   the   voice   of   the LORD   full   of   splen - dor.

EmSUS2   Em   C   D   Am7   D

Verse 3

3. The   God   of glo - ry   thun-ders.   In his   tem-ple they all cry,   "Glo-ry!"   The

G   Gmaj7   CSUS2   C   A   A7   DSUS2   D

Ant.

LORD sits en-throned a-bove the   flood;   The   LORD   sits as king for - ev - er.

B   B7   EmSUS2   Em   C   D Am7   D

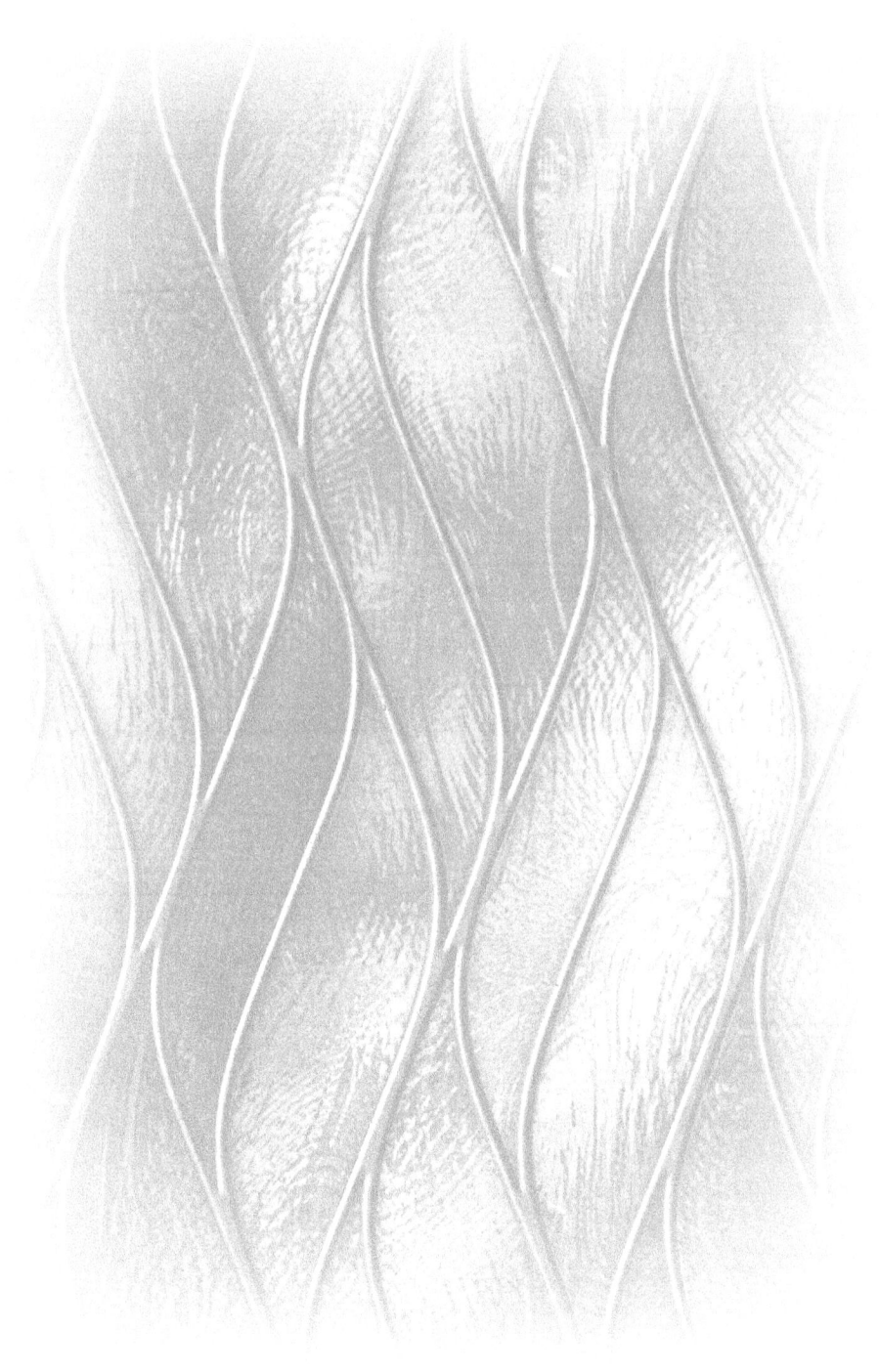

Psalm 51: Be Merciful, O Lord

First Sunday of Lent, Year A

Psalm 51:3-4, 5-6, 12-13, 17

Michael Joncas
Tone 4B: Individual Lament

First Sunday of Lent, Year A

First Sunday of Lent, Year A

First Sunday of Lent, Year A

Psalm 33: Lord, Let Your Mercy
Second Sunday of Lent, Year A

Psalm 33:4-5, 18-19, 20, 22

Michael Joncas
Tone 1B: Hymn of Praise
Motivation from History or Torah

Second Sunday of Lent, Year A

Ant.

LORD loves jus-tice and right, and his mer-ci-ful love fills the earth.

Verse 2

2. Yes, the LORD's eyes are on those who fear him, who hope in his mer-ci - ful

Ant.

love, to res-cue their soul from death, to keep them a-live in fam - ine.

Second Sunday of Lent, Year A

3. Our soul is wait-ing for the LORD. He is our help and our shield. May your

mer-ci-ful love be up-on us, as we hope in you, O LORD.

Psalm 95: If Today You Hear His Voice
Third Sunday of Lent, Year A

Psalm 95:1-2, 6-7, 8-9

Michael Joncas
Tone 1D: Processional

Text: Refrain, *Lectionary for Mass*, © 1969, 1997, ICEL;
Verses, *The Abbey Psalms and Canticles*, © 2010, 2018, United States Conference of Catholic Bishops, Washington, DC. All rights reserved.
Music: © 2023 The Jan Michael Joncas Trust. Published and administered by Liturgical Press, Collegeville, MN 56321. All rights reserved.

Third Sunday of Lent, Year A

Third Sunday of Lent, Year A

Third Sunday of Lent, Year A

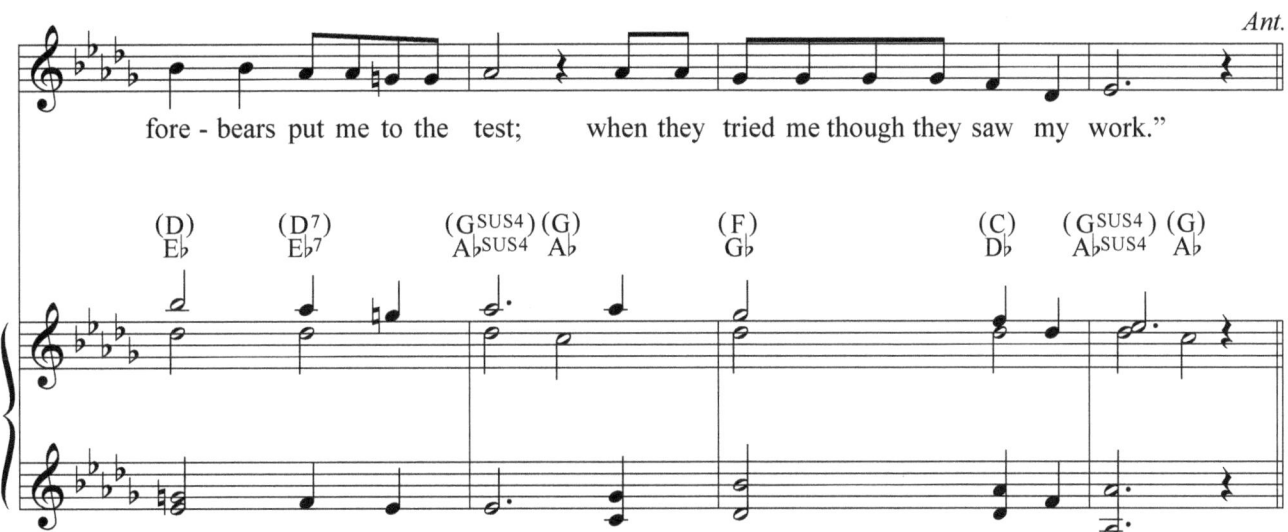

Psalm 23: The Lord Is My Shepherd
Fourth Sunday of Lent, Year A

Psalm 23:1-3a, 3b-4, 5, 6

Michael Joncas
Tone 6: Psalm of Confidence

Fourth Sunday of Lent, Year A

Fourth Sunday of Lent, Year A

Fourth Sunday of Lent, Year A

Psalm 130: With the Lord There Is Mercy

Fifth Sunday of Lent, Year A

Psalm 130:1-2, 3-4, 5-6, 7-8

Michael Joncas
Tone 4B: Individual Lament

Fifth Sunday of Lent, Year A

Fifth Sunday of Lent, Year A

Fifth Sunday of Lent, Year A

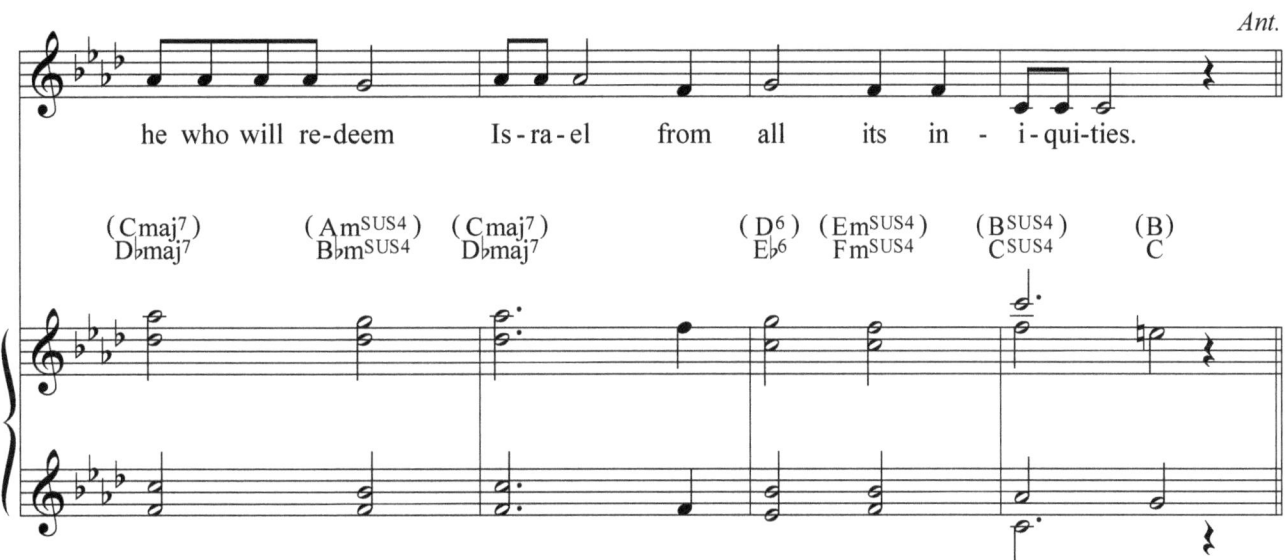

Psalm 118: Give Thanks to the Lord

Second Sunday of Easter/Divine Mercy Sunday, Years A, B, and C

Psalm 118:1-2, 16-17, 22-23

Michael Joncas
Tone 5B: Individual Thanksgiving

Antiphon

Joyfully ♩ = 80

Harmony: Al - le - lu - ia, al - le - lu - ia, al - le - lu - ia, al - le - lu - ia.

Melody: Give thanks to the Lord for he is good, his love is ev - er - last - ing.

Alternate Antiphon

Al - le - lu - ia, al - le - lu - ia, al - le - lu - ia, al - le - lu - ia.

Al - le - lu - ia, al - le - lu - ia, al - le - lu - ia, al - le - lu - ia.

Second Sunday of Easter/Divine Mercy Sunday, Years A, B, and C

Second Sunday of Easter/Divine Mercy Sunday, Years A, B, and C

Second Sunday of Easter/Divine Mercy Sunday, Years A, B, and C

Psalm 16: Lord, You Will Show Us

Third Sunday of Easter, Year A

Psalm 16:1-2, 5, 7-8, 9-10, 11

Michael Joncas
Tone 4C: Prayer for the Sick

Third Sunday of Easter, Year A

Third Sunday of Easter, Year A

Third Sunday of Easter, Year A

Psalm 23: The Lord Is My Shepherd
Fourth Sunday of Easter, Year A

Psalm 23:1-3a, 3b-4, 5, 6

Michael Joncas
Tone 6: Psalm of Confidence

Antiphon

Trustingly ♩ = 80

The Lord is my shep-herd; there is noth-ing I shall want.

Alternate Antiphon

Al-le-lu-ia, al-le-lu-ia, al-le-lu-ia.

Fourth Sunday of Easter, Year A

Fourth Sunday of Easter, Year A

Fourth Sunday of Easter, Year A

Verse 3

3. You have pre - pared a ta - ble be - fore me in the sight of my foes. My

Dm⁷   Am^SUS2 Am   D   D⁷   G^SUS4   G

Ant.

head you have a-noint-ed with oil; my cup is o - ver - flow - ing.

Am   F   Dm⁷   Am   C   G^SUS4   G

Verse 4

4. Sure - ly good-ness and mer-cy shall fol-low me all the days of my life. In the

Dm⁷   Am^SUS2 Am   D   D⁷   G^SUS4   G

Fourth Sunday of Easter, Year A

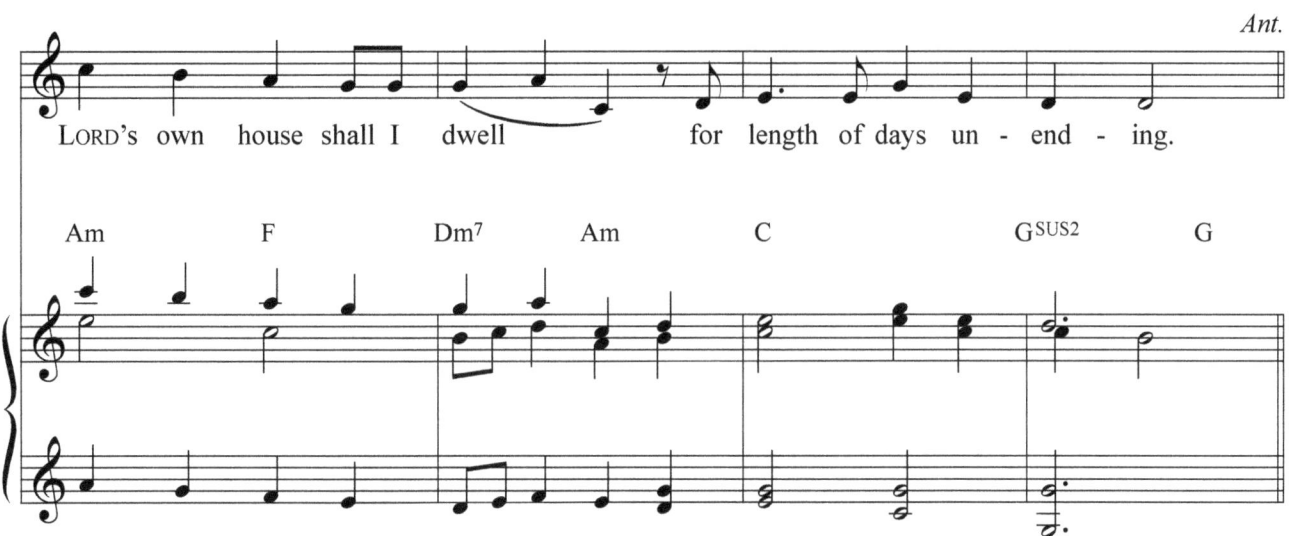

Psalm 33: Lord, Let Your Mercy
Fifth Sunday of Easter, Year A

Psalm 33:1-2, 4-5, 18-19

Michael Joncas
Tone 1B: Hymn of Praise
Motivation from History or Torah

Text: Refrain, *Lectionary for Mass*, © 1969, 1997, ICEL;
Verses, *The Abbey Psalms and Canticles*, © 2010, 2018, United States Conference of Catholic Bishops, Washington, DC. All rights reserved.
Music: © 2023 The Jan Michael Joncas Trust. Published and administered by Liturgical Press, Collegeville, MN 56321. All rights reserved.

Fifth Sunday of Easter, Year A

Fifth Sunday of Easter, Year A

Fifth Sunday of Easter, Year A

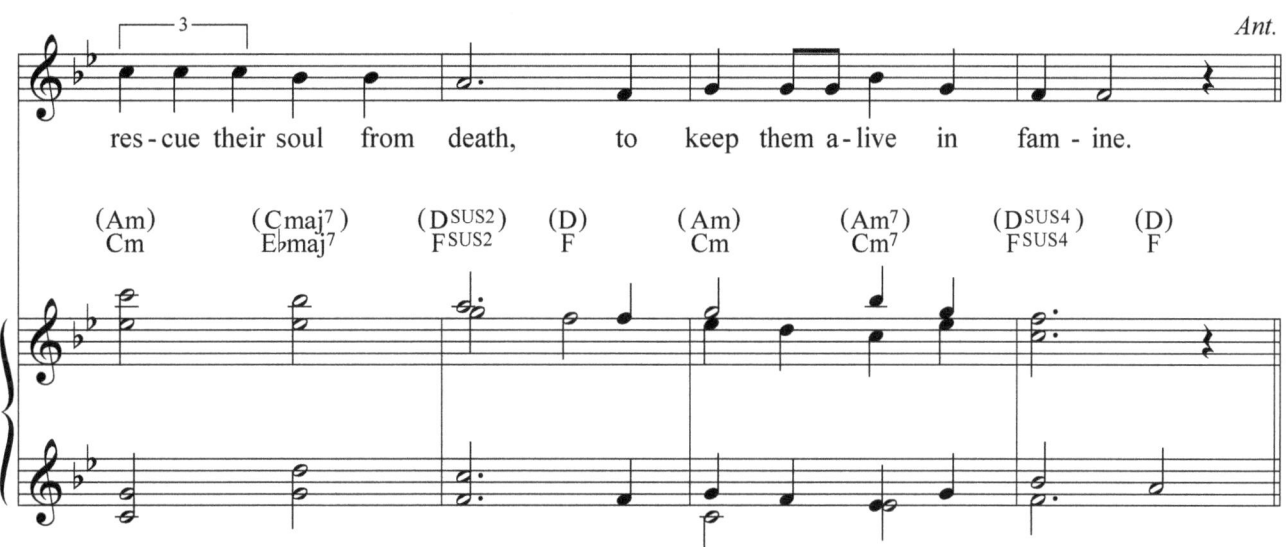

Psalm 66: Let All the Earth

Sixth Sunday of Easter, Year A

Psalm 66:1-3, 4-5, 6-7, 16, 20

Michael Joncas
Tone 5B: Individual Thanksgiving

Sixth Sunday of Easter, Year A

Sixth Sunday of Easter, Year A

Ant.

Come and see the works of God; his won-drous deeds a-mong the chil-dren of Ad-am.

G⁶   F♯⁷   Bm   D   Em   Em⁷   A^SUS4   A

Verse 3

3. He turned the sea in-to dry land; they passed through the riv-er on foot. Let our

D   D/C♯   D^SUS2   D   Em⁷   Dmaj⁷   A^SUS4   A

Ant.

joy, then, be in him; he rules for-ev-er by his might.

G⁶   F♯⁷   Bm   D   Em   Em⁷   A^SUS4   A

Sixth Sunday of Easter, Year A

Psalm 27: I Believe That I Shall See
Seventh Sunday of Easter, Year A

Psalm 27:1, 4, 7-8

Michael Joncas
Tone 6: Psalm of Confidence

Seventh Sunday of Easter, Year A

Seventh Sunday of Easter, Year A

Seventh Sunday of Easter, Year A

Psalm 40: Here Am I, Lord
Second Sunday in Ordinary Time, Year A

Psalm 40:2, 4, 7-8, 8-9, 10

Michael Joncas
Tone 5B: Individual Thanksgiving

Text: Refrain, *Lectionary for Mass*, © 1969, 1997, ICEL;
Verses, *The Abbey Psalms and Canticles*, © 2010, 2018, United States Conference of Catholic Bishops, Washington, DC. All rights reserved.
Music: © 2023 The Jan Michael Joncas Trust. Published and administered by Liturgical Press, Collegeville, MN 56321. All rights reserved.

Second Sunday in Ordinary Time, Year A

Second Sunday in Ordinary Time, Year A

Second Sunday in Ordinary Time, Year A

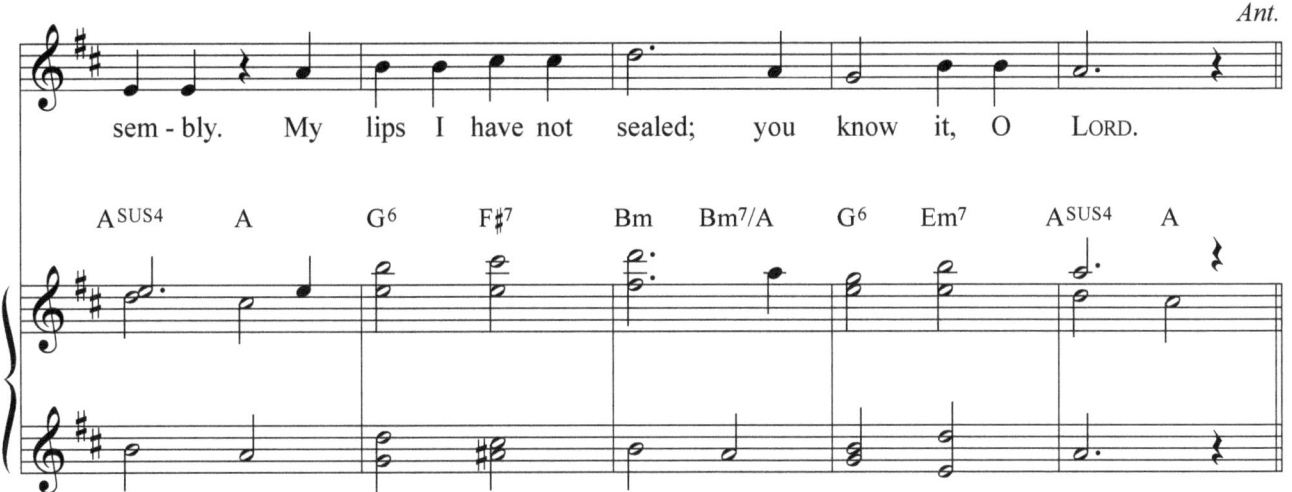

Psalm 27: The Lord Is My Light
Third Sunday in Ordinary Time, Year A

Psalm 27:1, 4, 13-14

Michael Joncas
Tone 6: Psalm of Confidence

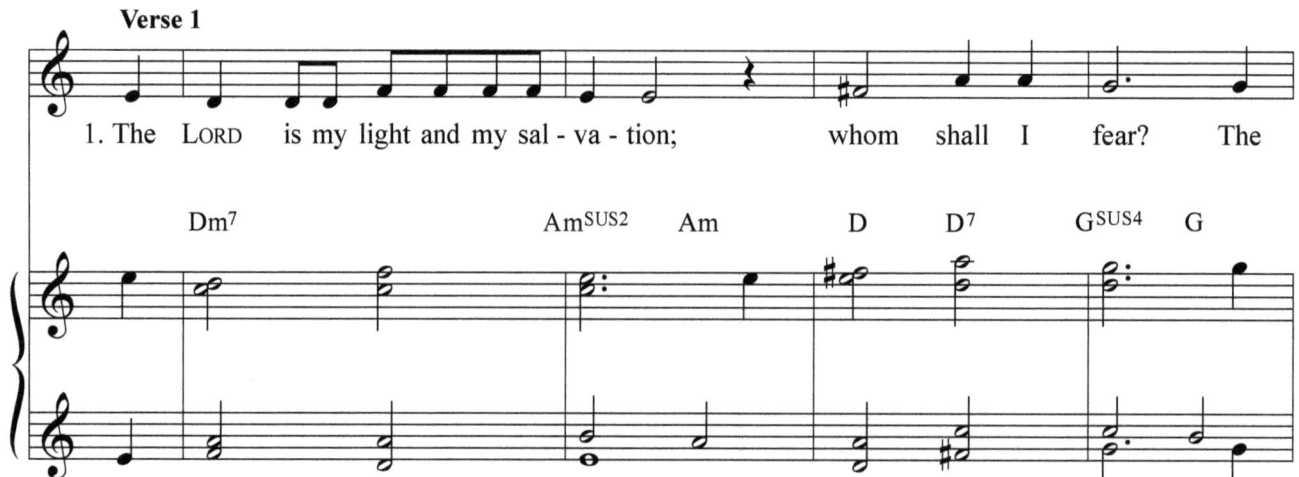

Third Sunday in Ordinary Time, Year A

Third Sunday in Ordinary Time, Year A

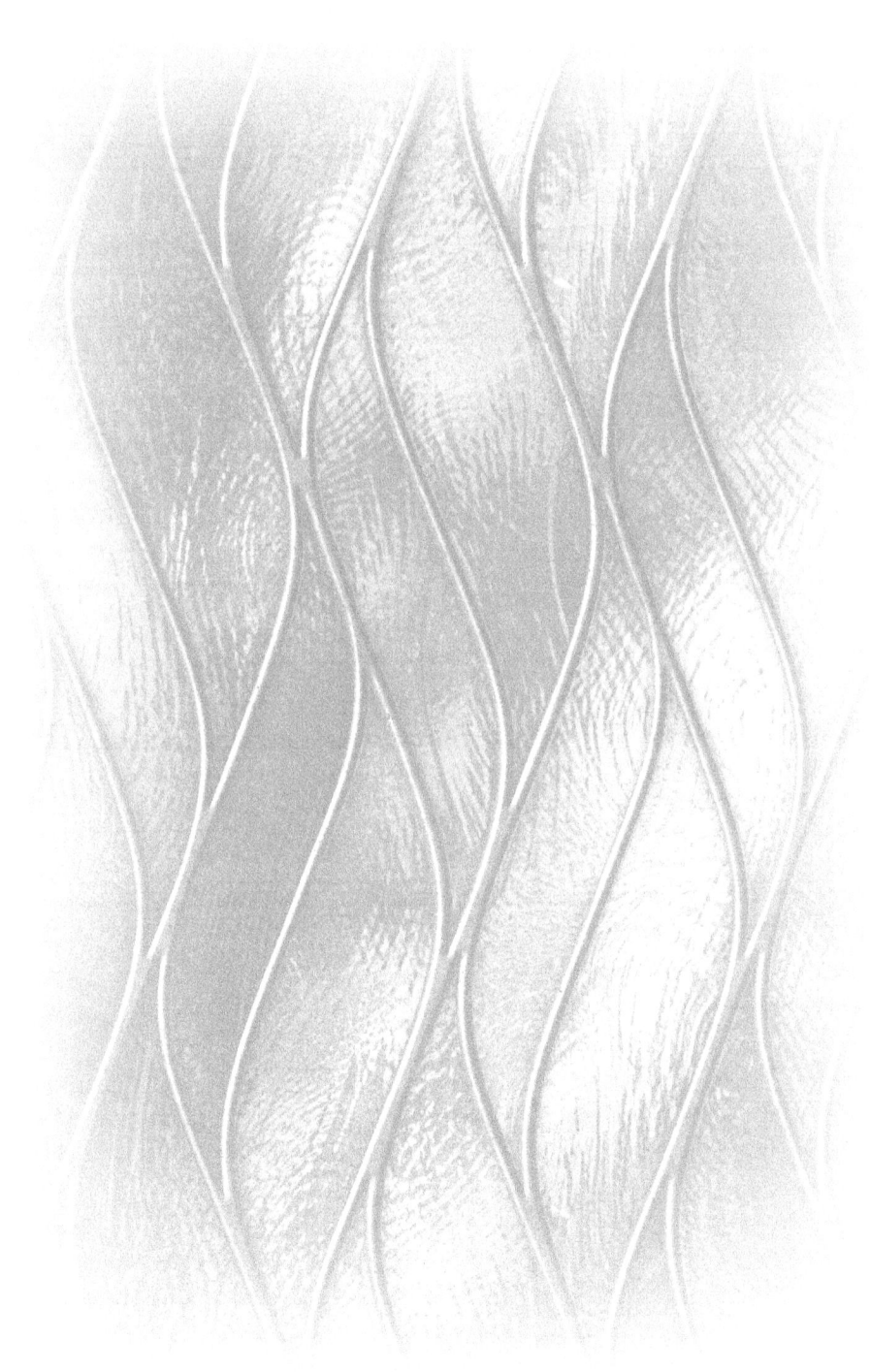

Psalm 146: Blessed Are the Poor
Fourth Sunday in Ordinary Time, Year A

Psalm 146:6-7, 8-9, 10

Michael Joncas
Tone 1B: Hymn of Praise
Motivation from History or Torah

Fourth Sunday in Ordinary Time, Year A

Fourth Sunday in Ordinary Time, Year A

Fourth Sunday in Ordinary Time, Year A

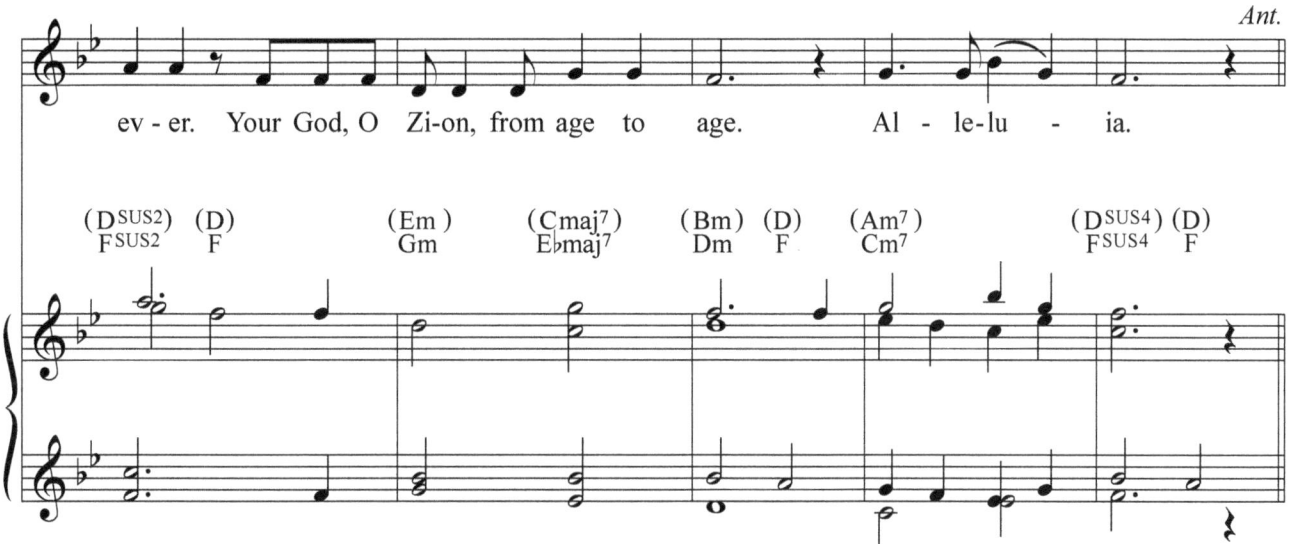

Psalm 112: The Just Man Is a Light

Fifth Sunday in Ordinary Time, Year A

Psalm 112:4-5, 6-7, 8-9

Michael Joncas
Tone 8A: Wisdom Psalm 1

Text: Refrain, *Lectionary for Mass*, © 1969, 1997, ICEL;
Verses, *The Abbey Psalms and Canticles*, © 2010, 2018, United States Conference of Catholic Bishops, Washington, DC. All rights reserved.
Music: © 2023 The Jan Michael Joncas Trust. Published and administered by Liturgical Press, Collegeville, MN 56321. All rights reserved.

Fifth Sunday in Ordinary Time, Year A

Fifth Sunday in Ordinary Time, Year A

Fifth Sunday in Ordinary Time, Year A

Psalm 119: Blessed Are They Who Follow

Sixth Sunday in Ordinary Time, Year A

Psalm 119:1-2, 4-5, 17-18, 33-34

Michael Joncas
Tone 8A: Wisdom Psalm 1

Sixth Sunday in Ordinary Time, Year A

Sixth Sunday in Ordinary Time, Year A

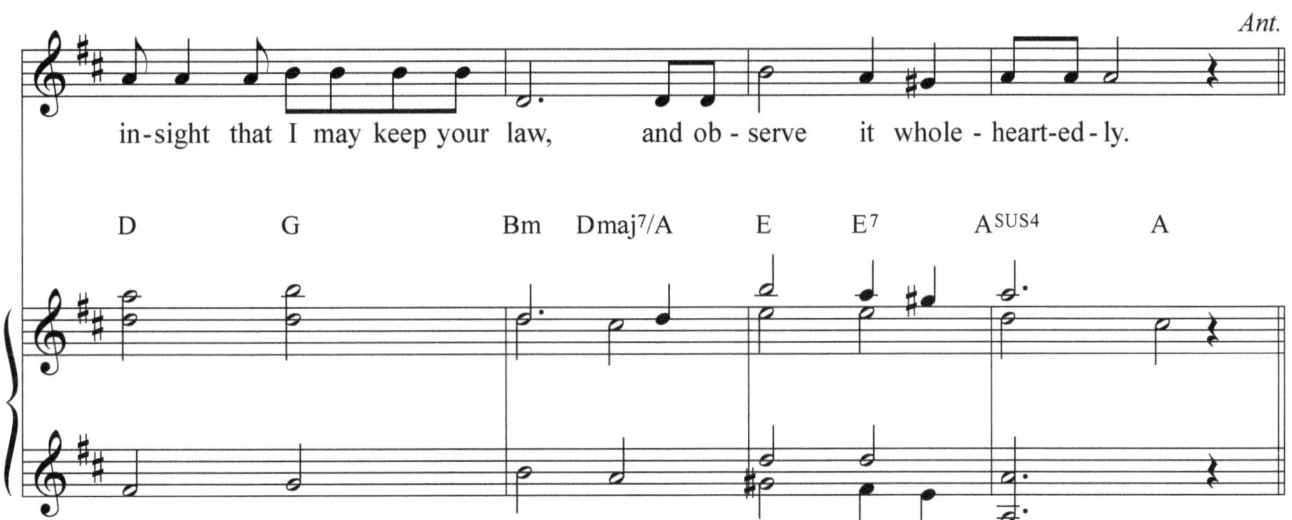

Psalm 103: The Lord Is Kind
Seventh Sunday in Ordinary Time, Year A

Psalm 103:1-2, 3-4, 8, 10, 12-13

Michael Joncas
Tone 5B: Individual Thanksgiving

Seventh Sunday in Ordinary Time, Year A

Seventh Sunday in Ordinary Time, Year A

Seventh Sunday in Ordinary Time, Year A

Psalm 62: Rest in God Alone
Eighth Sunday in Ordinary Time, Year A

Psalm 62:2-3, 6-7, 8-9

Michael Joncas
Tone 6: Psalm of Confidence

Antiphon

Gently ♩ = 80

Harmony

Rest in God a - lone, my soul; rest in God a - lone.

Melody

Rest in God a - lone, my soul; rest in God a - lone.

Am   F   Dm⁷   Am   C/G   G   C

Verse 1

1. In God a - lone is my soul at rest; my sal - va-tion comes from him. He a-

Dm⁷   Am^SUS2 Am   D   D⁷   G^SUS4   G

Eighth Sunday in Ordinary Time, Year A

Eighth Sunday in Ordinary Time, Year A

Psalm 31: Lord, Be My Rock
Ninth Sunday in Ordinary Time, Year A

Psalm 31:2-3, 3-4, 17, 25

Michael Joncas
Tone 4C: Prayer for the Sick

Ninth Sunday in Ordinary Time, Year A

Ninth Sunday in Ordinary Time, Year A

Psalm 50: To the Upright
Tenth Sunday in Ordinary Time, Year A

Psalm 50:1, 8, 12-13, 14-15

Michael Joncas
Tone 3: Prophetic Psalm

Text: Refrain, *Lectionary for Mass*, © 1969, 1997, ICEL;
Verses, *The Abbey Psalms and Canticles*, © 2010, 2018, United States Conference of Catholic Bishops, Washington, DC. All rights reserved.
Music: © 2023 The Jan Michael Joncas Trust. Published and administered by Liturgical Press, Collegeville, MN 56321. All rights reserved.

Tenth Sunday in Ordinary Time, Year A

Tenth Sunday in Ordinary Time, Year A

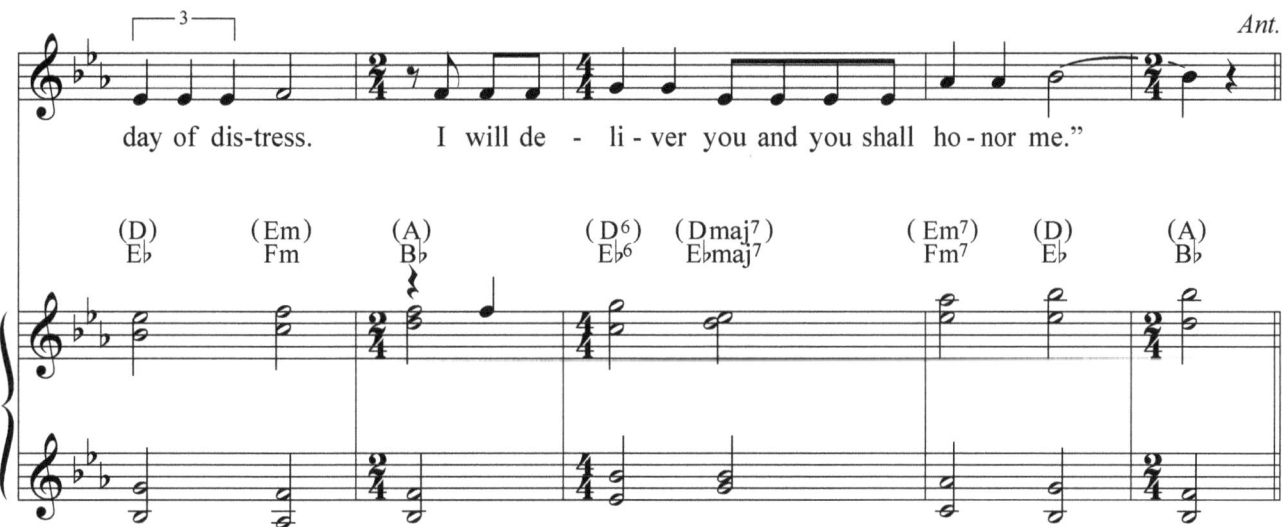

Ant.

day of dis-tress.   I will de - li - ver you and you shall ho - nor me."

Psalm 100: We Are His People

Eleventh Sunday in Ordinary Time, Year A

Psalm 100:1-2, 3, 5

Michael Joncas
Tone 1D: Processional

Eleventh Sunday in Ordinary Time, Year A

Eleventh Sunday in Ordinary Time, Year A

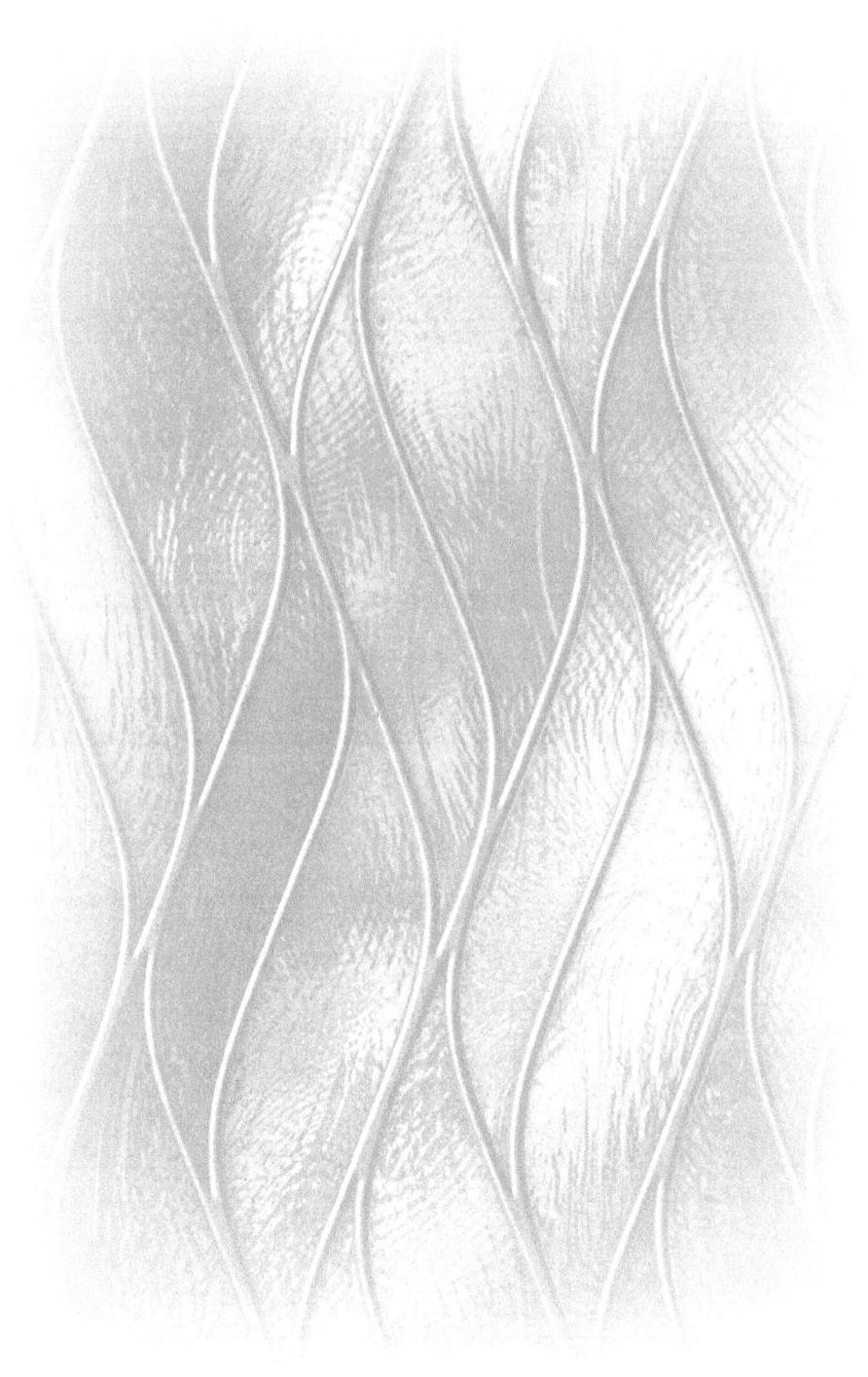

Psalm 68: Lord, in Your Great Love
Twelfth Sunday in Ordinary Time, Year A

Psalm 67:8-10, 14, 17, 33-35

Michael Joncas
Tone 4B: Individual Lament

Twelfth Sunday in Ordinary Time, Year A

Twelfth Sunday in Ordinary Time, Year A

Ant.

Psalm 89: For Ever I Will Sing
Thirteenth Sunday in Ordinary Time, Year A

Psalm 89:2-3, 16-17, 18-19

Michael Joncas
Tone 1E: Hymn of Praise
to YHWH as King

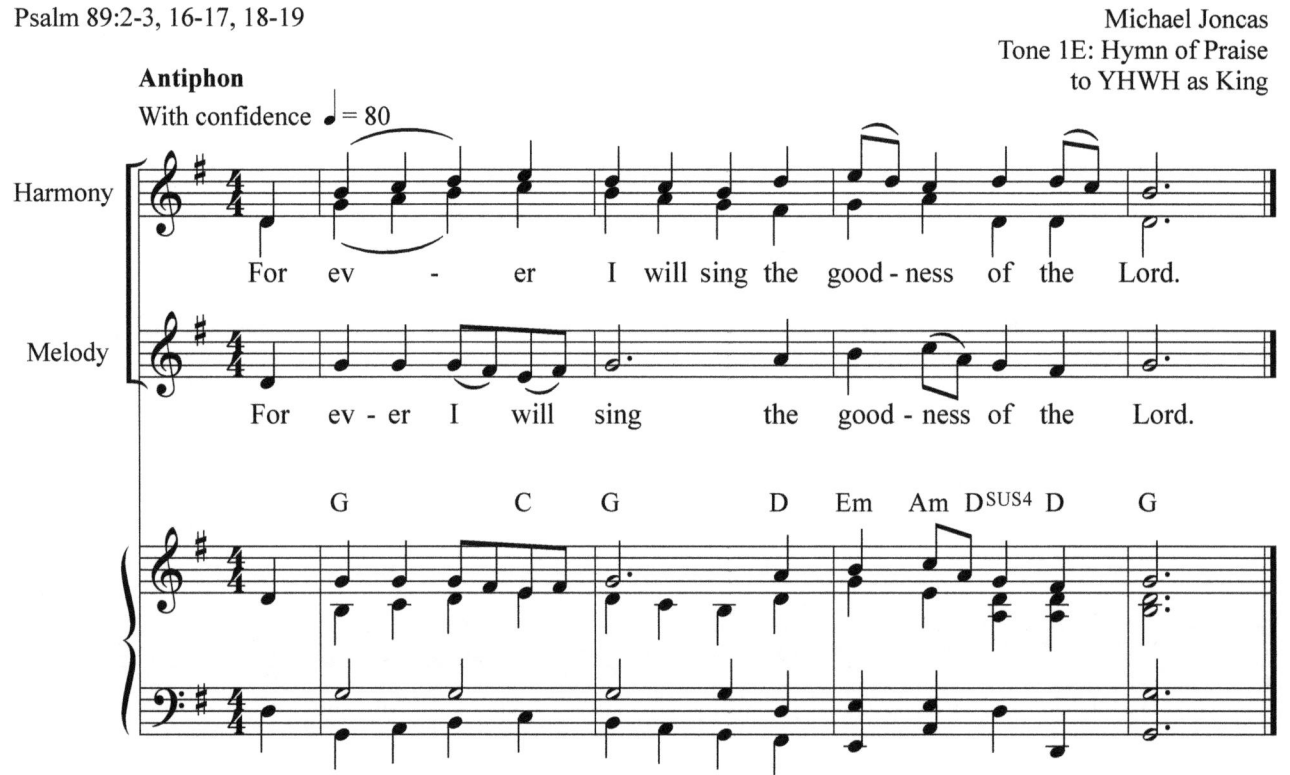

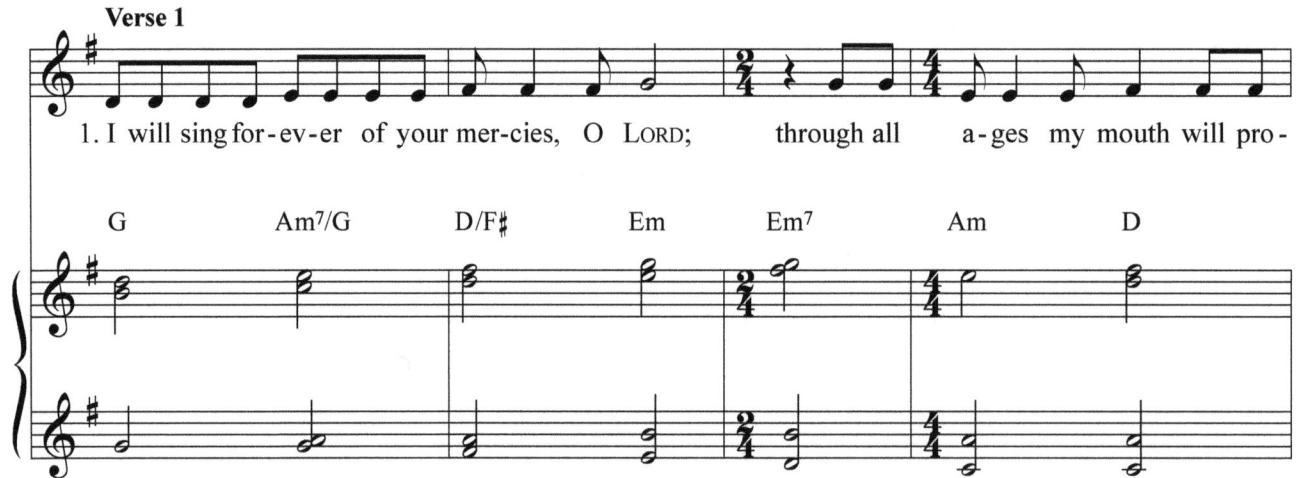

Thirteenth Sunday in Ordinary Time, Year A

Thirteenth Sunday in Ordinary Time, Year A

Thirteenth Sunday in Ordinary Time, Year A

Psalm 145: I Will Praise Your Name For Ever

Fourteenth Sunday in Ordinary Time, Year A

Psalm 145:1-2, 8-9, 10-11, 13-14

Michael Joncas
Tone 1B: Hymn of Praise
Motivation from History or Torah

Fourteenth Sunday in Ordinary Time, Year A

Psalm 145: I Will Praise Your Name For Ever, pg. 3

Fourteenth Sunday in Ordinary Time, Year A

Fourteenth Sunday in Ordinary Time, Year A

Verse 4

4. The Lord is faith-ful in all his words, and ho-ly in all his deeds. The Lord sup-

ports all who fall, and rais-es up all who are bowed down.

Psalm 65: The Seed That Falls
Fifteenth Sunday in Ordinary Time, Year A

Psalm 65:10, 11, 12-13, 14

Michael Joncas
Tone 5A: Communal Thanksgiving

Fifteenth Sunday in Ordinary Time, Year A

Fifteenth Sunday in Ordinary Time, Year A

Fifteenth Sunday in Ordinary Time, Year A

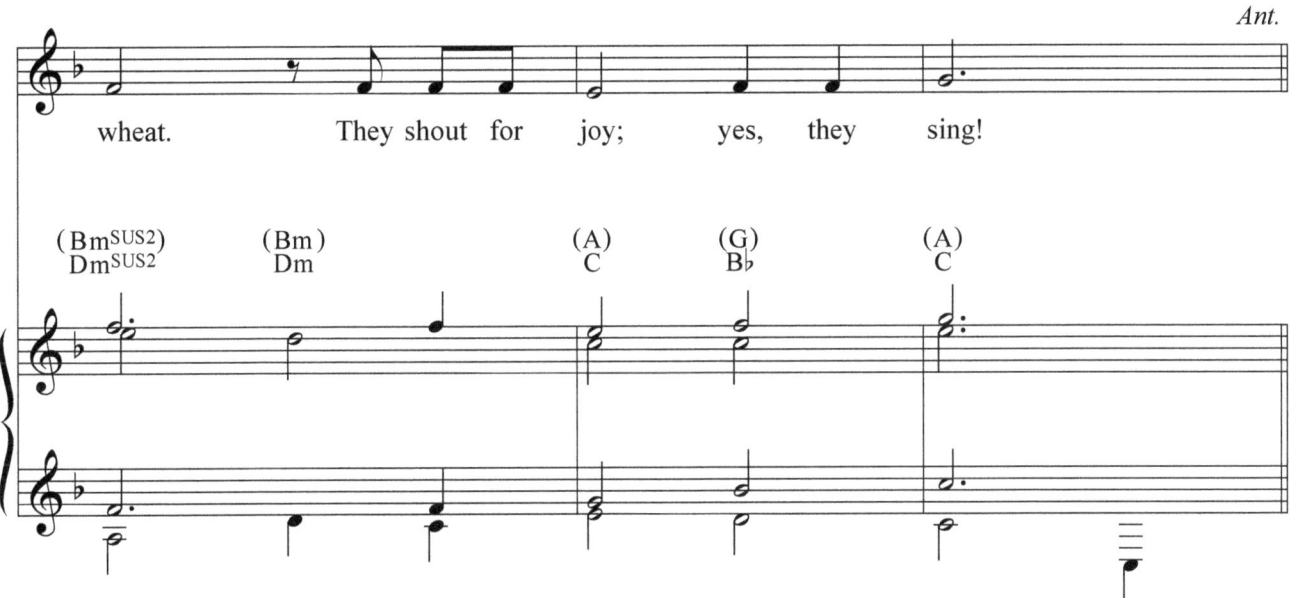

Psalm 86: Lord, You Are Good and Forgiving
Sixteenth Sunday in Ordinary Time, Year A

Psalm 86:5-6, 9-10, 15-16

Michael Joncas
Tone 4B: Individual Lament

Antiphon

With conviction ♩ = 85

Harmony

Lord, Lord, you are good, good and for - giv - ing.

Melody

Lord, you are good, good and for - giv - ing.

Verse 1

1. O Lord, you are good and for-giv-ing, full of mer-cy to all who call to you. Give

Sixteenth Sunday in Ordinary Time, Year A

Sixteenth Sunday in Ordinary Time, Year A

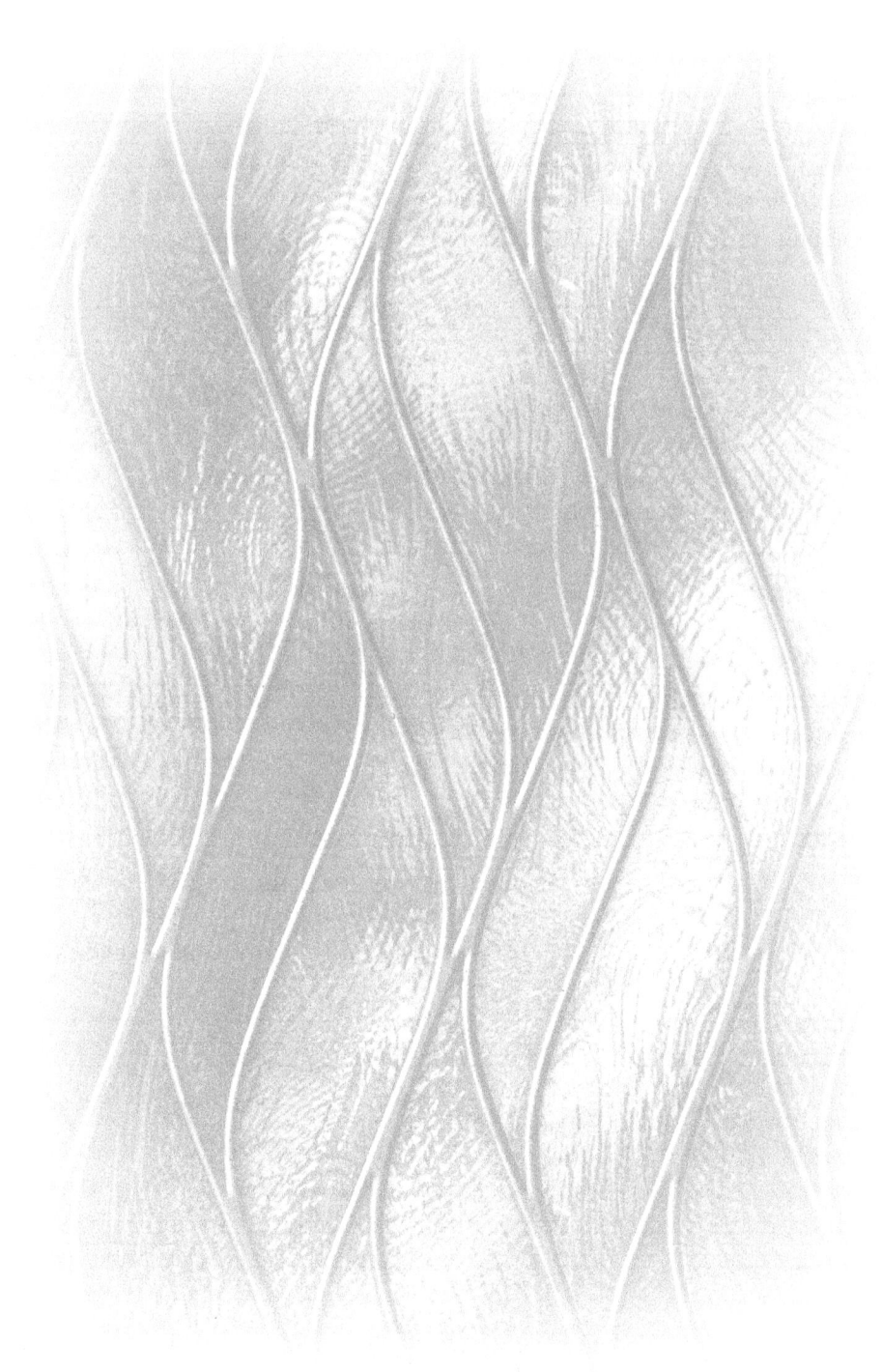

Psalm 119: Lord, I Love Your Commands
Seventeenth Sunday in Ordinary Time, Year A

Psalm 119:57, 72, 127-128, 129-130

Michael Joncas
Tone 8A: Wisdom Psalm 1

Seventeenth Sunday in Ordinary Time, Year A

Seventeenth Sunday in Ordinary Time, Year A

Verse 4

4. Your de-crees are won-der-ful in-deed; there-fore my soul o - beys them. The un-

D   A/C♯   Bm   D   Em⁷   D   A   A/G

Ant.

fold-ing of your word gives light, and un-der - stand-ing to the sim - ple.

D   G   Bm   Dmaj⁷/A   E   E⁷   A^SUS4   A

Psalm 145: The Hand of the Lord

Eighteenth Sunday in Ordinary Time, Year A

Psalm 145:8-9, 15-16, 17-18

Michael Joncas
Tone 1B: Hymn of Praise
Motivation from History or Torah

Eighteenth Sunday in Ordinary Time, Year A

Psalm 85: Lord, Let Us See Your Kindness

Nineteenth Sunday in Ordinary Time, Year A

Psalm 85:9-10, 11-12, 13-14

Michael Joncas
Tone 3: Prophetic Psalm

Nineteenth Sunday in Ordinary Time, Year A

Nineteenth Sunday in Ordinary Time, Year A

Psalm 67: O God, Let All the Nations Praise You
Twentieth Sunday in Ordinary Time, Year A

Psalm 67:2-3, 5, 6, 8

Michael Joncas
Tone 5A: Communal Thanksgiving

Twentieth Sunday in Ordinary Time, Year A

Twentieth Sunday in Ordinary Time, Year A

Twentieth Sunday in Ordinary Time, Year A

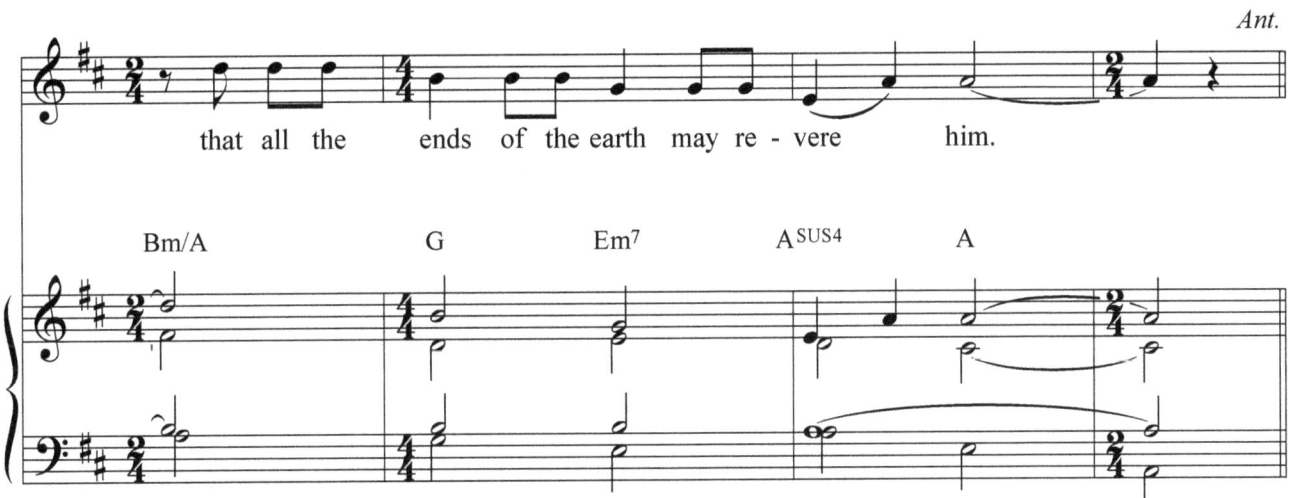

that all the   ends of the earth may re - vere   him.

Psalm 138: Lord, Your Love Is Eternal
Twenty-First Sunday in Ordinary Time, Year A

Psalm 138:1-2, 2-3, 6, 8

Michael Joncas
Tone 5B: Individual Thanksgiving

Antiphon

Thankfully ♩ = 80

Harmony

Lord, your love is e-ter - nal; do not for-sake the work of your hands.

Melody

Lord, your love is e-ter-nal; do not for-sake the work of your hands.

D   Em⁷ A   D   G   A   D

Verse 1

1. I thank you, LORD, with all my heart; you have heard the words of my mouth. In the

D   D/C♯   D^SUS2 D   Em⁷   D/C♯   A^SUS4 A/G

Twenty-First Sunday in Ordinary Time, Year A

Twenty-First Sunday in Ordinary Time, Year A

Psalm 63: My Soul Is Thirsting for You
Twenty-Second Sunday in Ordinary Time, Year A

Psalm 63:2, 3-4, 5-6, 8-9

Michael Joncas
Tone 4B: Individual Lament

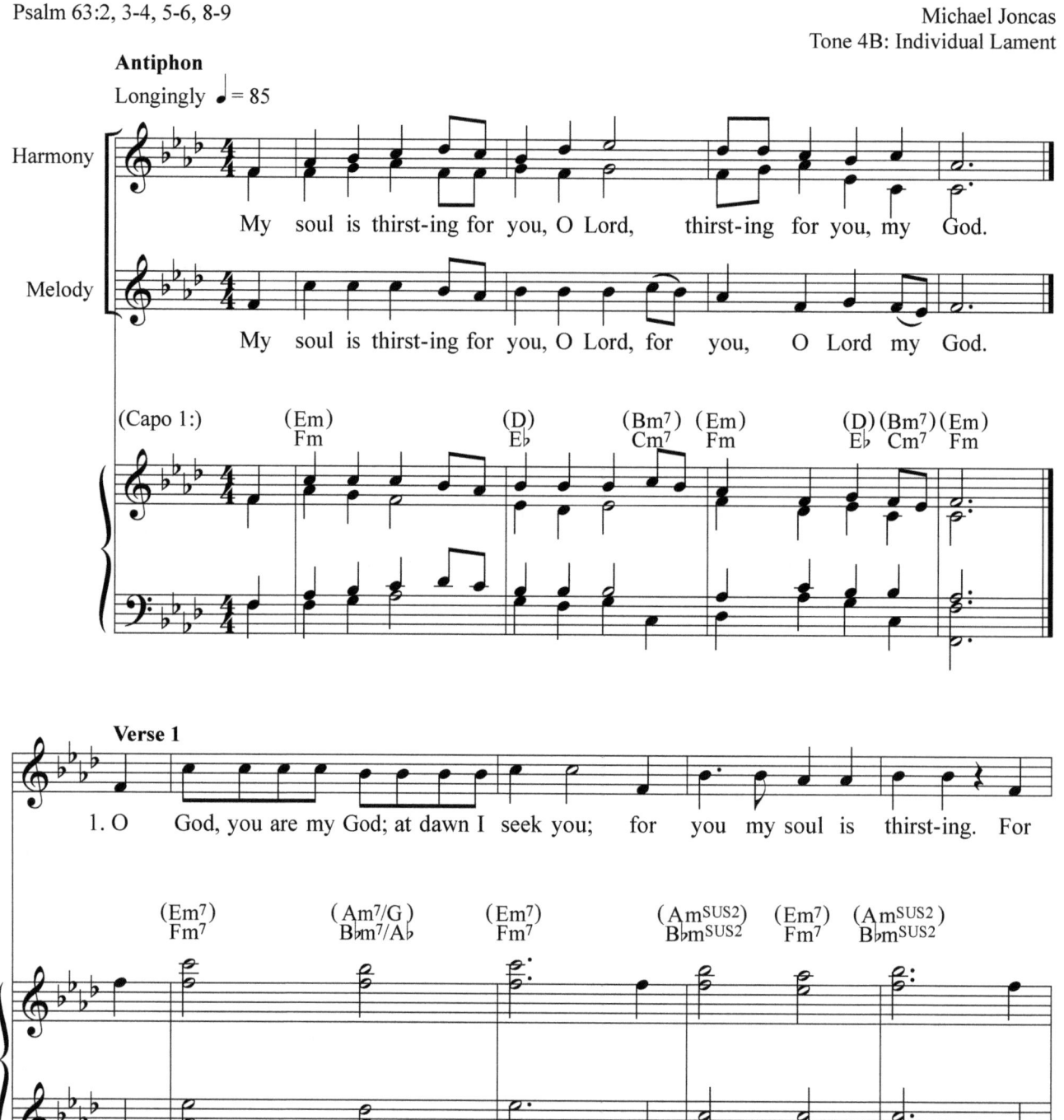

Twenty-Second Sunday in Ordinary Time, Year A

Twenty-Second Sunday in Ordinary Time, Year A

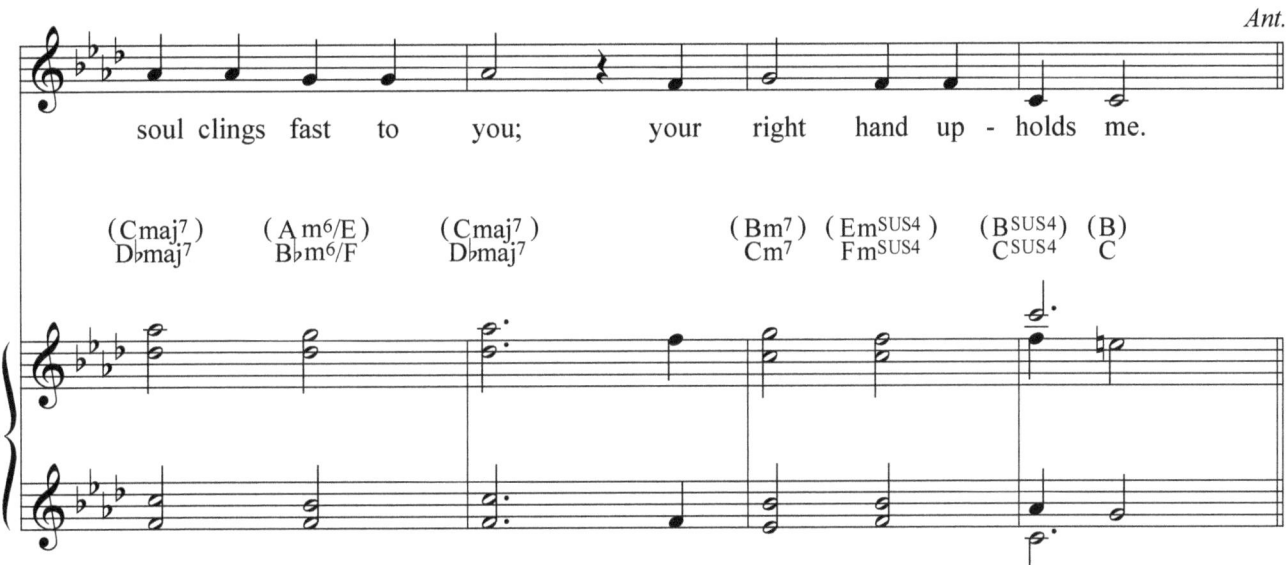

Psalm 95: If Today You Hear His Voice
Twenty-Third Sunday in Ordinary Time, Year A

Psalm 95:1-2, 6-7, 8-9

Michael Joncas
Tone 1D: Processional

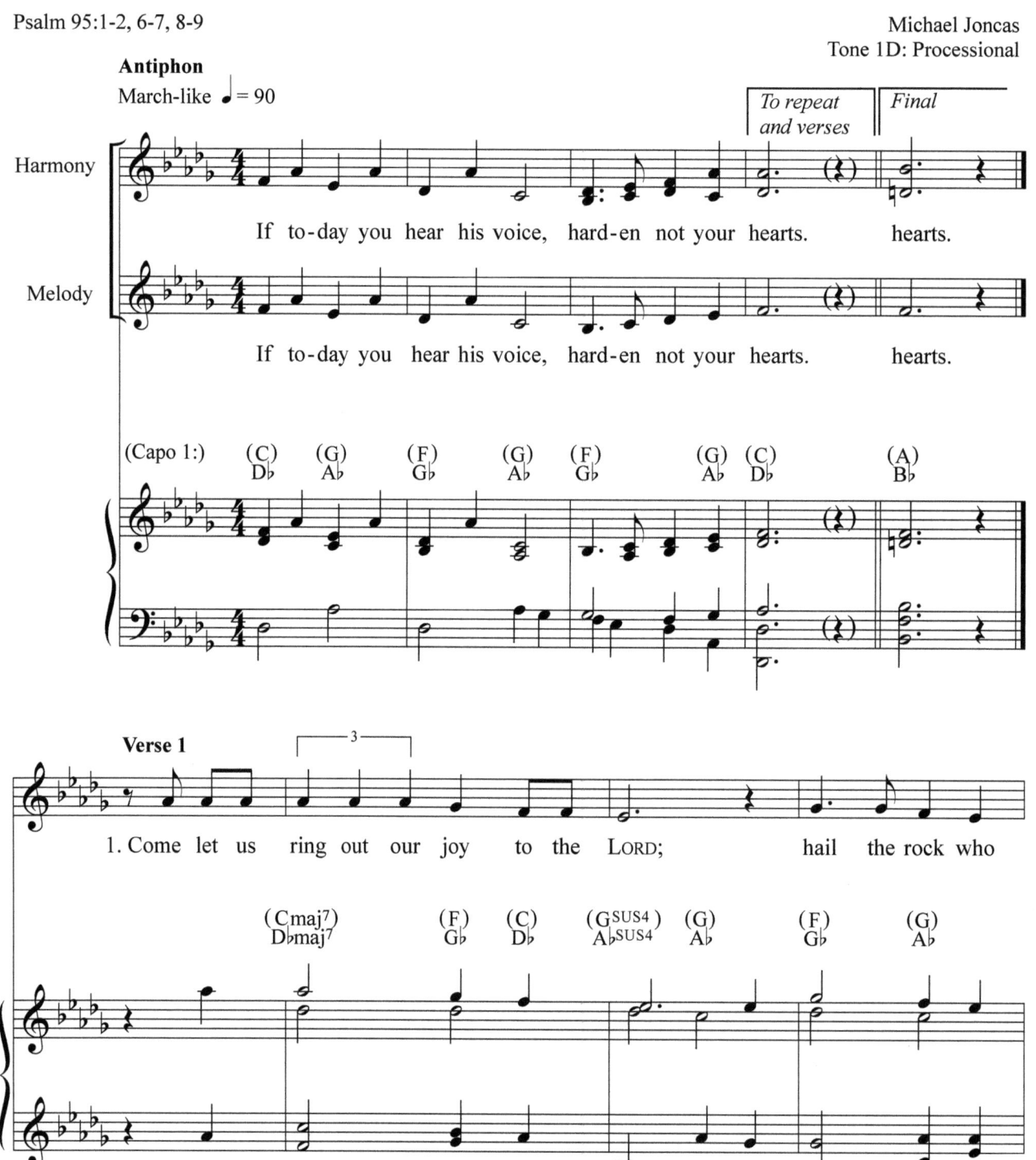

Twenty-Third Sunday in Ordinary Time, Year A

Twenty-Third Sunday in Ordinary Time, Year A

Twenty-Third Sunday in Ordinary Time, Year A

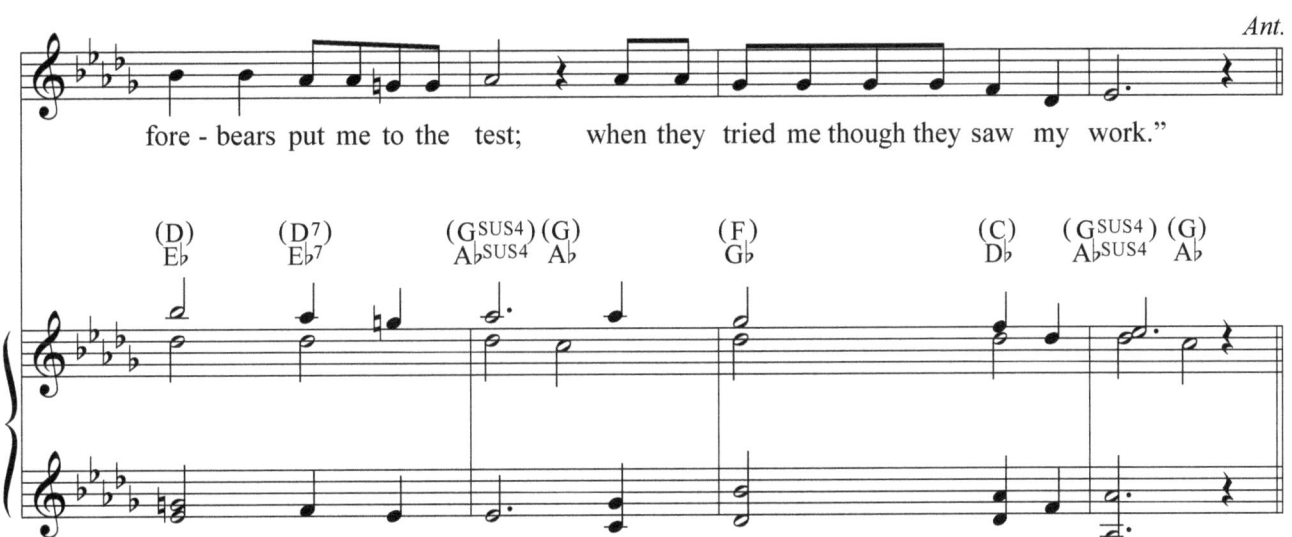

Psalm 103: The Lord Is Kind and Merciful
Twenty-Fourth Sunday in Ordinary Time, Year A

Psalm 103:1-2, 3-4, 9-10, 11-12

Michael Joncas
Tone 5B: Individual Thanksgiving

Twenty-Fourth Sunday in Ordinary Time, Year A

name.   Bless the LORD, O my soul,   and   nev-er   for-get   all his   be - ne - fits.

Verse 2

2. It   is   the   LORD   who for-gives   all   your   sins,   who   heals   ev-'ry one of your

ills,   who re - deems your life from the   grave,   who   crowns you with mer-cy and com-

Twenty-Fourth Sunday in Ordinary Time, Year A

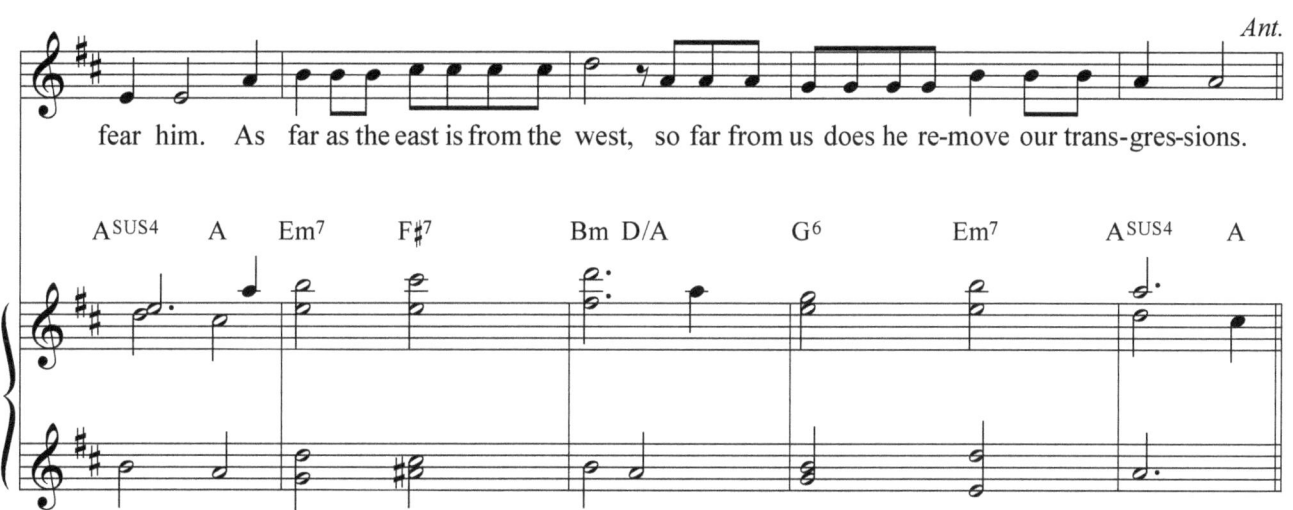

Psalm 145: The Lord Is Near
Twenty-Fifth Sunday in Ordinary Time, Year A

Psalm 145:2-3, 8-9, 17-18

Michael Joncas
Tone 1B: Hymn of Praise
Motivation from History or Torah

Twenty-Fifth Sunday in Ordinary Time, Year A

Twenty-Fifth Sunday in Ordinary Time, Year A

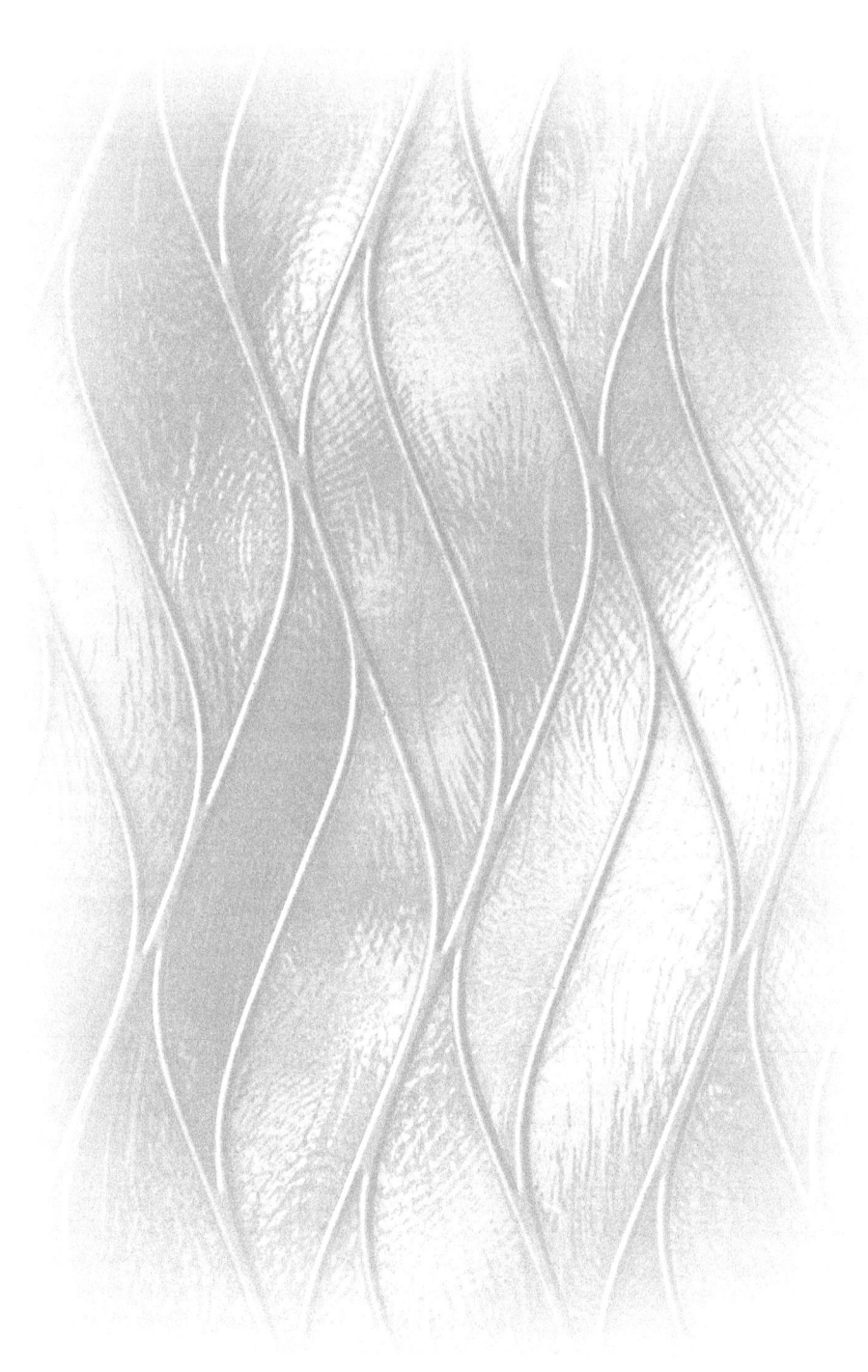

Psalm 25: Remember Your Mercies, O Lord
Twenty-Sixth Sunday in Ordinary Time, Year A

Psalm 25:4-5, 6-7, 8-9

Michael Joncas
Tone 8A: Wisdom Psalm 1

Twenty-Sixth Sunday in Ordinary Time, Year A

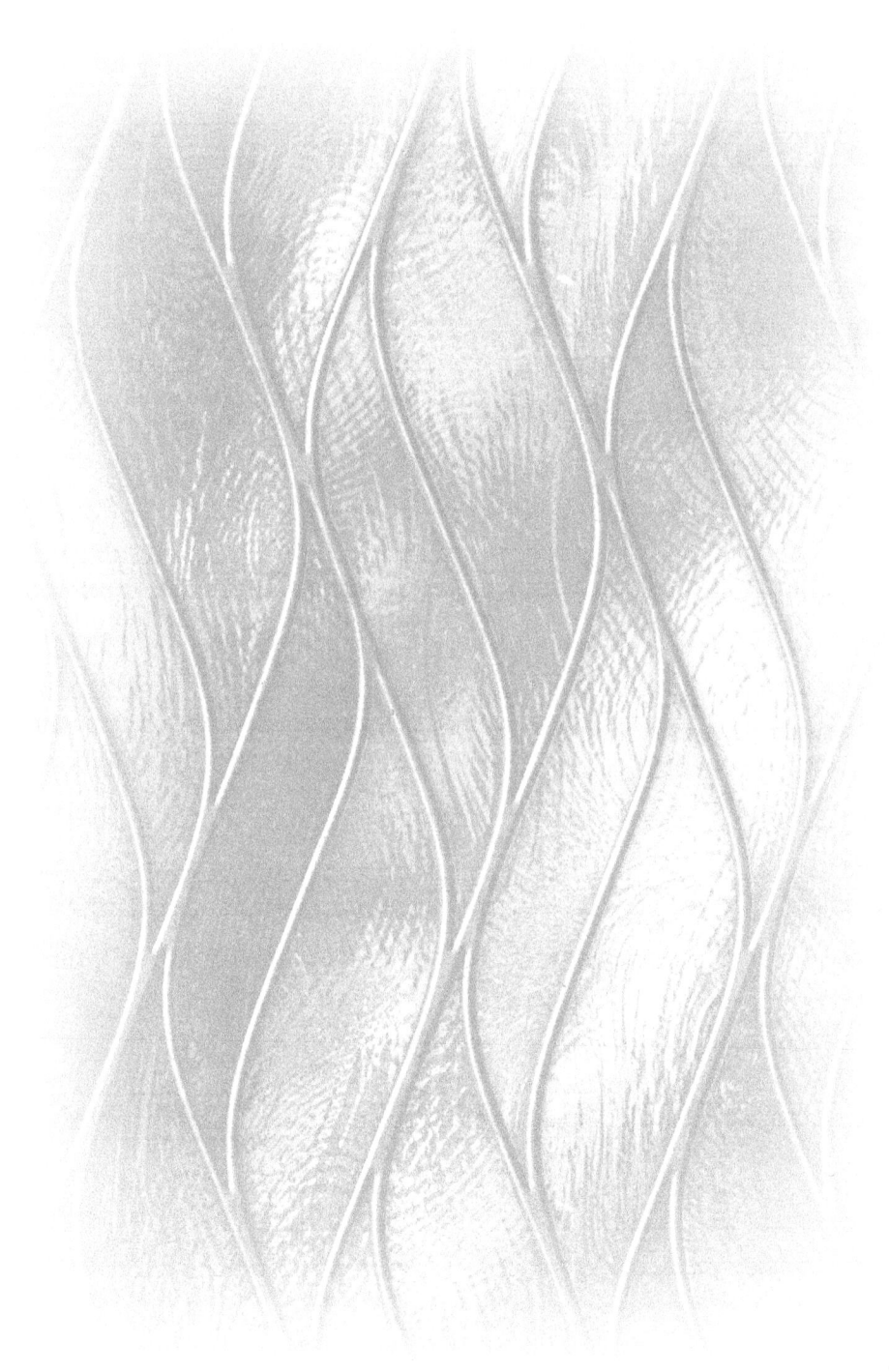

Psalm 80: The Vineyard of the Lord
Twenty-Seventh Sunday in Ordinary Time, Year A

Psalm 80:9, 12, 13-14, 15-16, 19-20

Michael Joncas
Tone 4A: Community Lament

Antiphon
Pleading ♩ = 85

Harmony: The vine-yard of the Lord is the house of Is - ra - el.

Melody: The vine-yard of the Lord is the house of Is - ra - el.

Em | Bm | A | D | Em

Verse 1

1. You brought a vine out of E-gypt; you drove out the na-tions and plant-ed it. It

Em | D/E | Em | D⁶ | Am/F♯ | D⁶

Twenty-Seventh Sunday in Ordinary Time, Year A

Twenty-Seventh Sunday in Ordinary Time, Year A

Psalm 23: I Shall Live in the House of the Lord
Twenty-Eighth Sunday in Ordinary Time, Year A

Psalm 23:1-3a, 3b-4, 5, 6

Michael Joncas
Tone 6: Psalm of Confidence

Twenty-Eighth Sunday in Ordinary Time, Year A

Twenty-Eighth Sunday in Ordinary Time, Year A

Twenty-Eighth Sunday in Ordinary Time, Year A

Psalm 96: Give the Lord Glory
Twenty-Ninth Sunday in Ordinary Time, Year A

Psalm 96:1, 3, 4-5, 7-8, 9-10

Michael Joncas
Tone 1E: Hymn of Praise
to YHWH as King

Twenty-Ninth Sunday in Ordinary Time, Year A

Twenty-Ninth Sunday in Ordinary Time, Year A

Twenty-Ninth Sunday in Ordinary Time, Year A

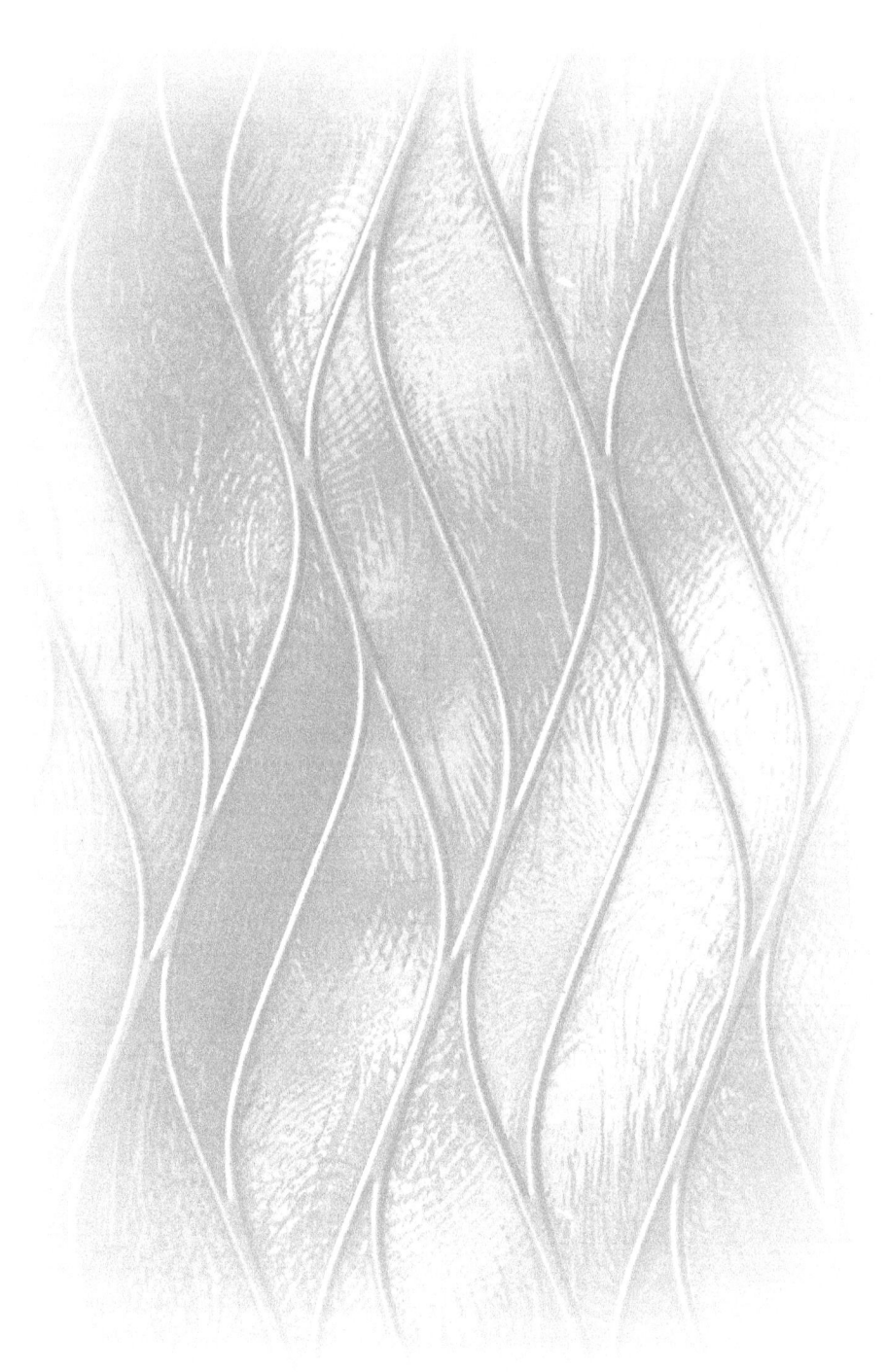

Psalm 18: I Love You, Lord, My Strength
Thirtieth Sunday in Ordinary Time, Year A

Psalm 18:2-3, 3-4, 47, 51

Michael Joncas
Tone 2C: Royal Davidic
Song of Thanksgiving

Thirtieth Sunday in Ordinary Time, Year A

Thirtieth Sunday in Ordinary Time, Year A

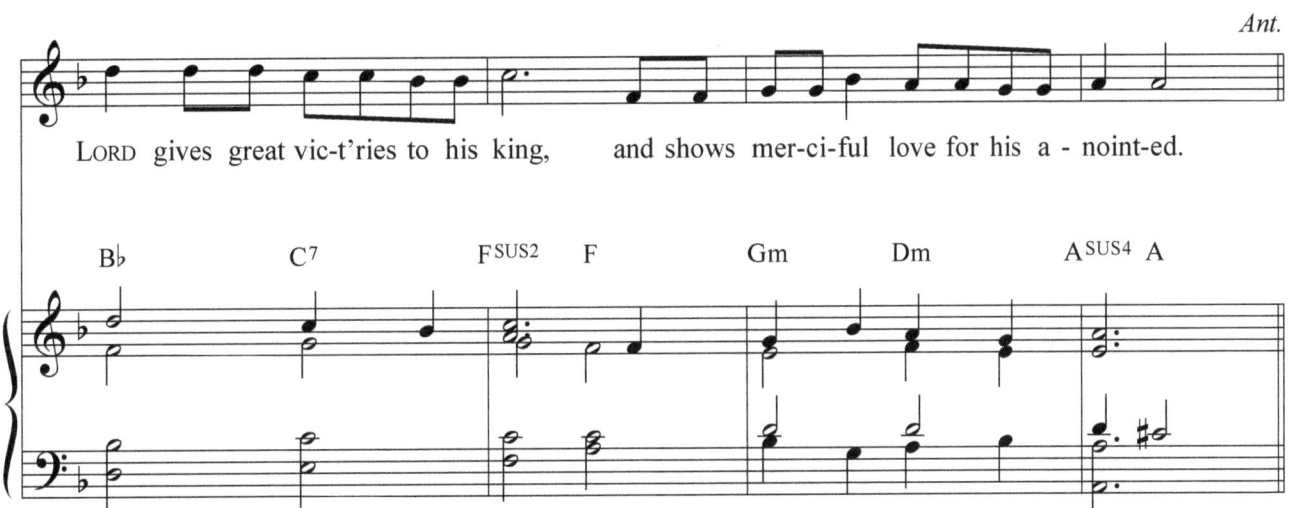

Psalm 131: In You, Lord, I Have Found My Peace
Thirty-First Sunday in Ordinary Time, Year A

Psalm 131:1, 2, 3

Michael Joncas
Tone 6: Psalm of Confidence

Thirty-First Sunday in Ordinary Time, Year A

Psalm 63: My Soul Is Thirsting for You
Thirty-Second Sunday in Ordinary Time, Year A

Psalm 63:2, 3-4, 5-6, 7-8

Michael Joncas
Tone 4B: Individual Lament

Thirty-Second Sunday in Ordinary Time, Year A

Thirty-Second Sunday in Ordinary Time, Year A

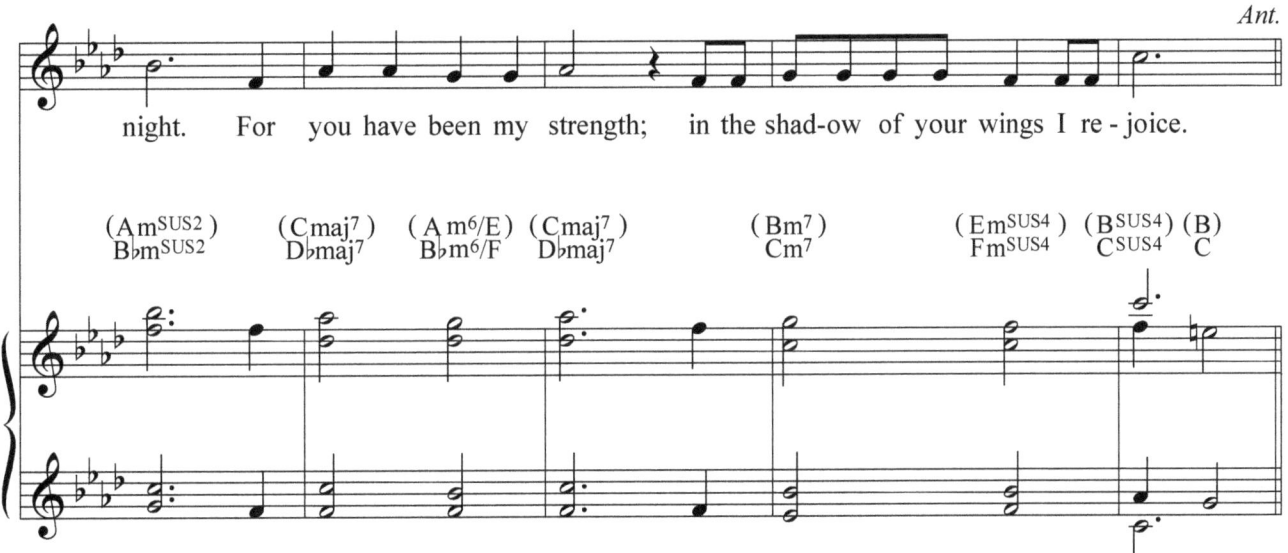

200

Psalm 128: Blessed Are Those
Thirty-Third Sunday in Ordinary Time, Year A

Psalm 128:1-2, 3, 4-5

Michael Joncas
Tone 8B: Wisdom Psalm 2

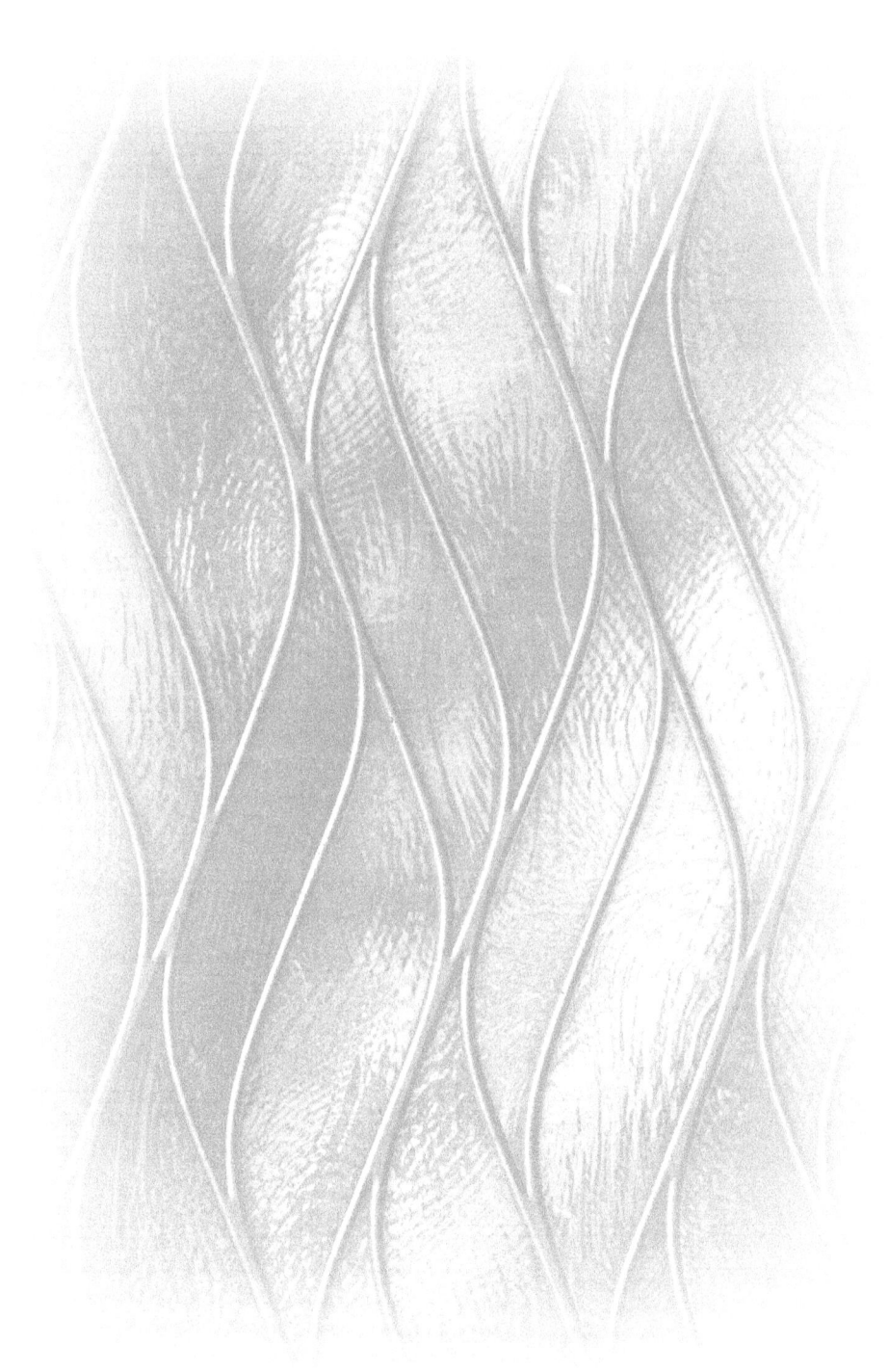

Psalm 23: The Lord Is My Shepherd

Solemnity of Christ the King/Thirty-Fourth Sunday in Ordinary Time, Year A

Psalm 23:1-2, 2-3, 5-6

Michael Joncas
Tone 6: Psalm of Confidence

Antiphon

Trustingly ♩ = 80

Harmony

The Lord is my shep - herd; there is no-thing I shall want.

Melody

The Lord is my shep - herd; there is no-thing I shall want.

Am F Dm⁷ Am C G C

Verse 1

1. The LORD is my shep-herd; there is no - thing I shall want.

Dm⁷ F Am^SUS2 Am D D⁷ G^SUS4 G

Solemnity of Christ the King/Thirty-Fourth Sunday in Ordinary Time, Year A

Solemnity of Christ the King/Thirty-Fourth Sunday in Ordinary Time, Year A

Solemnity of Christ the King/Thirty-Fourth Sunday in Ordinary Time, Year A